SEVEN SECRETS

of an

EMOTIONALLY INTELLIGENT COACH

SCOTT R. LIVINGSTON

**Buttermilk
Ridge
Publishing**

Published by:
Buttermilk Ridge Publishing
136 S. 9th Street, Ste 18
Noblesville, IN 46060
www.buttermilkridgepublishing.com

Distributed by:
IntegratEI
17437 Carey Road, #224
Westfield, IN 46074
www.IntegratEI.com

Library of Congress Control Number: 2009930546

Livingston, Scott Robert
    Seven Secrets of an Emotionally Intelligent Coach / Scott R. Livingston
        p.   cm.
    ISBN 978-0-9723961-2-8

Front cover photo by Artsem Martysiuk
Back cover photo by Lori Koppold.

A portion of the proceeds from the sale of this book go to further the leadership development goals of International Faith Initiatives' Mentorship Program in the former Soviet Union.

Printed in the USA

Printed on acid-free paper

Dedication

This book is dedicated to my family.

To Kim, my wife - you are an amazing individual, uniquely gifted by God with such empathy and compassion for others that no emotional intelligence assessment tool could ever measure. Your patience with me is endless. Your passion to see me succeed is unequaled. I am eternally in your service. I love you.

To Zach, Gretchen and Gregory - you are the three best kids a dad could ever hope for or be blessed with. You have allowed me, over the years, to practice my coaching as a father. Thank you for allowing me to fail. It is in these times where I have failed in my coaching skills as a dad that you were able to teach me about forgiveness. I love you.

Acknowledgments

Many people had input in making this book possible, and there are a few I would like to thank by name.

First, this work would not have been possible without the tireless efforts of Mike Linville. Mike served as my coach and my editor through this, my inaugural voyage in writing. A special crown is reserved in heaven for Mike. His patience with me was amazing. He was flexible with deadlines, as just about everything I wrote took longer than I expected. Thank you, Mike, for your diligence and attention to detail.

The idea for this book came in a conversation with Kevin Yaney, whose company is responsible for publishing this work. Kevin, you are an amazing inspiration. You kept me going when things got tough in the writing process. Thank you for your belief in the work I am doing.

I would also like to thank all those who allowed me to interview them, both coaches and those who have been coached by others. Without you and your stories, this book would have been just theory. You brought these concepts and ideas to life.

There are several people to thank from my previous career at Eli Lilly. This is where I first became interested and developed my passion for coaching. There are many amazing coaches in that organization, individuals who started me on my journey. Terry Chandler, Tom Considine, Jerry Gorski, Rick Morris, Doug Opel: you guys have experienced more about coaching than I will ever know. Your wisdom in the coaching arena is endless. Your encouragement and support of me as I made the transition from industry to entrepreneur will always be valued and treasured.

From this same great company, I would also like to thank

my sales teams from Peoria and St. Louis. You all allowed me to practice and hone my skills as a coach. Thank you for your patience and for allowing me to grow my leadership skills at your expense.

JP Pawliw-Fry and Bill Benjamin, from the Institute for Health and Human Potential, your combined wisdom, expertise and practical training approach to emotional intelligence lit the spark for this exciting topic that still burns in me to this day. Thank you for your philosophy on abundance and your willingness to share learning to grow humanity. You have both been great encouragers and coaches over the years. Thank you.

Many thanks to Jeremy Robinson who, as my coach, lives the integration of emotional intelligence and coaching. Jeremy, you will never realize the impact that your coaching has had on me. Your skill as a teacher, mentor, coach, and confidant has always given me practical, encouraging suggestions that have strengthened my belief in my own abilities. You are an amazing individual human being, and I am grateful to you for sharing your skills with me.

Contents

Foreword

In spite of the best intentions, most individuals who coach fail to have the impact they desire. They work very hard to do their best, to do everything the way they should and yet do not have the kind of impact they desire to have...and are left wondering why.

'Internal' coaches (that is, managers as coach) fail to achieve the success they desire because they fall into what is known as the "task trap". When pressure builds as they feel overwhelmed by the amount of work required of them and the diminishing amount of time to do it, they focus on just *getting things done*. They focus on task. Understandably, they become very efficient day to day and, in fact, do accomplish a great deal. Unfortunately, they start to do too much themselves or resort to telling directs what to do in such a way that they miss an opportunity to coach their people and to grow that person's and the organization's capabilities.

More than anything, they allow the pressure of time and the need to get things done to cause them to move to their 'default behavior,' which is to work even harder at task and even less on coaching and growing the skills of the important people on their team. In their minds, they don't have time to perform a luxury such as coaching, because there is simply too much to get done and not enough time!

This is precisely the place where emotional intelligence can begin to exert its influence. When managers are able to manage the pressure of getting things done, they have more of their minds (literally, more working memory) available to them to coach their directs. They have more patience to move at the pace of their directs (always slower because of the learning curve). Such managers can more readily access coaching models that work (such as the one in this book), and they can better understand what is going on with their direct reports that may be effecting their behavior and performance. In other words, they begin to understand the emotion that may be driving that person's behavior. This is *impossible* to do if a coach is unable to manage his or her own emotions or does not understand the power of emotions upon behavior and performance. This is the scientific basis for coaching with emotional intelligence, highly valuable knowledge and insights that are often lacking in books and resources about coaching.

The second trap more likely impacts the 'external' or professional coaches. These are the people who coach for a living. These coaches often fall into the context trap. In their coaching relationships, they fail to understand the context of what their coaching clients are facing. Because they have never 'been there,' they don't understand why clients have trouble following through on goals or actions. Because they exist outside the organization and may have never spent any time inside an organization, professional coaches commonly do not understand the social and political pressures that exist within an organization. For instance, they fail to understand how difficult it is for a coaching client to have a difficult conversation with an underperformer or an obtuse boss.

There is data to suggest, for example, that fewer than ten percent of physicians, nurses and other clinical staff directly confront their colleagues about their concerns. In a classic example, a group of eight anesthesiologists agree that a peer is dangerously incompetent, but they don't confront him. Instead, they go to great efforts to schedule surgeries for the sickest babies at times when he is not on duty. This problem has persisted for over five years.

The reality is that this type of social and political pressure is at work *at all times* in organizations and can subvert even the best intentioned and most highly disciplined individuals. Of course, it is not impossible for an external coach to understand context. Certainly the best of them do. But incorporating this knowledge means you have to coach at a different level – which is what this book is all about.

If you are not experiencing the impact you desire as a

coach, or if you are falling into one of these two traps, then this book is for you. This book offers something very *different* from the usual: experience *and* insight. This text reveals wisdom that can only come from working with terrible bosses and hard-to-manage direct reports such as Scott Livingston has done, and insights that can only come from someone who has spent a great deal of his life studying human behavior from a scientific perspective. This author has brought a fresh perspective to coaching that can help you make the kind of difference you want to make, in any setting in which you may find yourself.

More than anything, this is an immense contribution to the great books on coaching and influence in business today. But to benefit from this book, you must do more than just read this book. You must use it!

Dr. J.P. Pawliw-Fry
Founder, The Institute for Health and Human Potential

Introduction

The genesis for this book comes from my own internal battle with reconciling the skill and art of coaching to the application of contextual coaching models. The idea that somehow we can capture the depth of the human spirit by looking at a two-dimensional model, composed of arrows and words surrounded by boxes has, as a professional coach, left me feeling empty and inadequate with respect to improving the performance of other professionals.

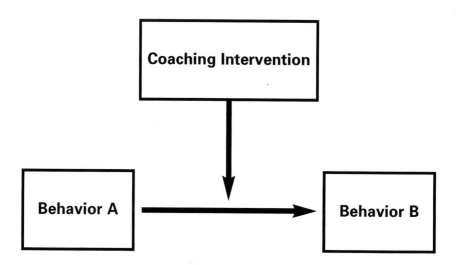

I can remember when I first saw a model for coaching (a little more complex than the one above but with the same logic) presented some ten years or so ago. My first thought was: *That is an interesting way to look at a process!* As I tried to apply this model to coaching situations with those on my team, I became exasperated! I was responsible for coaching others, with the goal of improving the work performance of the individuals on my team. Yet, for some reason, they just didn't want to fit themselves inside the little boxes on the model I had been taught. The barriers to change performance were always much more complex than the model I was using. The coaching model was perfect as a linear view of how a process could play out in theory, but was wholly inadequate for capturing the dynamics of the human spirit. My twenty (or so) years of coaching experience includes recreational baseball and soccer teams, a very high-performing sales team, and using coaching as a leadership tool within a training organization. Collectively, these experiences have led me to the conclusion that merely looking at a model for coaching, while vital to communicating a process, leaves out the most important part: the complexity of the human interaction.

The Hebrew Bible tells us that we are fearfully and wonderfully made. In this classic life instruction manual, we learn to be decent and true and not to be selfish. We learn to have self-control, to be patient and endure, to be humble, gentle and accepting of others. Perhaps most difficult of all, we are to love one another. It would seem that as a part of this creation standard, our emotions and feelings become a real barometer of how to measure behavior.

The emotional impact that the human spirit brings to coaching is what has been missing from the coaching models I have studied. As coaches, we work with people who have very real lives, not pieces of paper with a little ink splashed on them. When we ask the perfect open-ended question, as we've been taught to do, people don't always respond just like the model suggests, moving gracefully into the next box that has been carefully placed behind an arrow to show movement or progression.

This linear format is *not* how coaching has worked for me. I can remember times when I asked that perfect open-ended question that I thought would elicit the start of a behavior change conversation. My goal as a good coach, of course, was to take an employee's performance to the next level. Instead of getting that nice flow from "box to arrow to box" on a traditional coaching model, however, I got *tears!!!* *"That's not in the model I learned,"* I would think to myself, all the while wondering what my next word or action should be. Nowhere in the training for implementing such a model was any instruction on what to do if the other person cried …let alone equipping me to deal with the questions about what *I might have done* to create such a response. Those nonthreatening questions, true to the textbook in both form and fashion, which were meant to stimulate great conversation and the kind of change that would make any supervisor proud, instead made the person I was coaching cry. Many of those I interviewed in the writing of this book told similar stories. *You probably have one of your own!*

Take a moment to reflect upon this yourself. Do you have a coaching story or situation that you expected would go well, only to see it take a disastrous turn? If so, please share it with us. Simply access our website at: www.IntegratEI.com and click on "coaching story."

This book attempts to answers the question that traditionally has not been answered in corporate boardrooms, MBA programs, at undergraduate universities or traditional coach training programs. When the question is posed about how we move our careers forward and how we grow our organizations, the answers tend to revolve around the acquisition of new technical skills or abilities. But what if getting to the next level isn't about learning new facts and figures or implementing the latest management philosophy?

Recently, three universities in the southeastern region of the United States examined their undergraduate and graduate business programs. These institutions asked the following question of employers that were recruiting on their campuses: "What are the skills and talents you most need from our graduates?" The responses were quite surprising. Interpersonal skills, communication and team work were highly valued, as was leadership. Employers talked about things like vision, passion, and innovation.

As a result, the universities reviewed their curricula in order to determine if they were teaching what the recruiting companies expected graduates to possess. While the schools found that there were isolated courses that dealt minimally with some of the aforementioned subjects, the reality was stark. There were no classes dealing with communication skills in business and no classes on how to work together in a team. Perhaps it goes with saying that there were no courses that taught anything about vision, passion, or innovation.

So, if we aren't going to learn these valuable skills or acquire this essential knowledge within the walls of our universities or business schools, how do we improve needed skills such as coaching? How do we help vault our organizations to the next level of performance? In the pages of this book, we will explore the coupling of two very important disciplines in an effort to answer these critical questions.

There are some assumptions about you, the reader, that as an author I have made. Presumably, you are in a coaching role as a part of your job description. Likely, you are working with employees in business, government or non-profit. You may be an executive who feels the pressure to increase the productivity of the business unit for which you are responsible. You may be a supervisor who simply wants your people to do what they are being paid to do. Maybe you are a professional coach who consults and advises others in helping them to grow personally and professionally. You might be a professional advisor, like a physician, accountant, lawyer or engineer, who is simply trying to better connect with those in your organization in an effort to improve outcomes. You might even be a dad or a mom who coaches a recreational sports team.

As I reflect on these diverse areas in which coaching can be utilized for improving outcomes, perhaps most important of all are your kids. You might be a mom or dad who is trying to connect and build trust with your children. You've tried telling them what to do, but they just won't listen. Have you considered incorporating coaching skills into your parenting armamentarium? Wherever you may be on this spectrum of coaching opportunity, there is much for you to reflect and take action on inside these pages. Likely, this book may be different from others you may have read on coaching. *Seven Secrets of the Emotionally-Intelligent Coach* not only is intended to be an exercise of your intellect, but also an action plan to help you improve your coaching skills. Complete the exercises. Spend some time reflecting not upon what you think you would like to do or how you would like to be some day, but how you really are today. Write down examples of how you behave as a coach. Measure your progress and catch yourself getting better at the skills that really matter, those that characterize an *emotionally intelligent* coach.

Finally, a word about how this work is organized. There are three basic sections. The first third of this book will make the case for coaching fundamental skills in life and in business. If you lead anyone in any capacity, you are going to be asking them to do something that achieves a goal. Coaching is a skill to help you along this journey. The second third of the book discusses the role of emotional intelligence (EI), and its relevance to coaching is explored. You will learn what emotional intelligence is and the value it can bring when integrated into coaching skills. Then, through primarily observational study and behavioral interviews, seven important efficiencies are identified that will be useful for any coach to develop. The last section of this book leads you from intellect to action. A step-by-step action plan will be presented for you to develop the seven secrets of an emotionally intelligent coach.

While I readily acknowledge that additional scientific rigor needs to follow these initial observations as they relate to coaching, no doubt you will find that incorporating these efficiencies into your relationships will result in better and more productive coaching outcomes.

Best wishes as you develop coaching skills by learning and assimilating these *Seven Secrets of an Emotionally Intelligent Coach.*

PART I

Fundamental Coaching Skills

Why Won't They Just Do What I Tell Them To Do?

A colleague of mine named Tom relates the following story: *"Years ago, I was in charge of my company's customer service department, which included a group of designers and production people within our firm. We produced a certain kind of printed product for our clients, as well as handled some marketing and advertising for them. Daily deadlines were a fact of life. Meeting them meant we all had done what our clients expected of us; missing them was a disaster because it meant that we were letting our clients down. Each afternoon at 4:45, the courier would show up for our daily shipments. Our deadline was quite unforgiving. Missing the deadline meant that the work was destined to be a day late."*

"Then one day, we learned that Susan's husband had contracted cancer, too late to really treat it. Unfortunately, his condition deteriorated very quickly and within three months, he passed away. After three decades of marriage, naturally, Susan was devastated. She took some time off to grieve, during which I brought in a temporary worker to help do at least a portion of her job. The temp couldn't handle the workload and the pressure, and quit

after two days. In the month that Susan was gone, I mostly did my job and her job."

"I was so relieved the day that Susan came back to work. I remember thinking that I could finally get back to only doing ONE job around the office instead of two. As usual, the day was filled with a good deal of pressure which only mounted as the 4:45 deadline approached. Fully expecting Susan to help us meet our obligations to our clients that day, I was surprised to look up and see Susan standing at my desk and sobbing uncontrollably. At that moment I was on the telephone with a customer, assuring them that their job would go out the door that day. All the while, Susan starts blubbering something like, 'I can't do it, I can't do it, I can't do it.' Lots of thoughts started running through my mind, like, 'What am I going to do? We're five minutes from deadline and this stuff absolutely HAS to go out the door. If you're going to fall to pieces on me, why can't it be a half hour from now? I can't do your job in five minutes and my job too, and you can see I'm busy; you can see I'm talking with people. Why can't you just do what I need you to do?!'"

"In that moment, I was quite conflicted. I simply opened my mouth and said, 'Susan, I don't know what to say to you right now. Go back to your desk.' I was very dismissive of her. Hanging up the phone, I then did the best I could do to get that day's production out the door. But I felt absolutely horrible about it afterwards."

Tom asked the question that countless other managers and executives regularly ask themselves: "Why can't my people just do what I tell them to do?" It's an age-old dilemma, really, but one for which few people have discovered the answer. If you think Tom's story is an isolated incident, think again! Fully thirty percent of supervisors admit to ignoring employees on a daily basis. I happen to know that Tom took this situation particularly hard because he is a person of faith, one whom I personally know to be a very considerate person of others' feelings. And yet, though many years have passed since Tom's story about Susan occurred, he still remembers it vividly. Why? Because his working relationship with Susan was permanently damaged.

What would you have done in Tom's situation? Likely, you have been in a similar predicament yourself at one time or another. How did you handle it?

Today, eleven years later, Tom has come to see why his exchange with Susan had such a bad outcome. In a short amount of time, she had lost a man whom she had been married to for thirty years. Prior to her husband's illness, they had planned out their future retirement to Florida together. All of sudden, however, Susan had no idea what was going to happen next. She really didn't know what her future looked like. Everything that she had always thought was going to happen, wasn't going to happen anymore. Susan was scared.

Tom can recall the whole thing like it was yesterday, because he sees it as a milestone in his career. He has come to recognize that putting an employee in that kind of position never had a good outcome. Forcing a person to choose a mundane, ordinary work task over a torrential flood of traumatic emotion is to clearly communicate a core value, that the work is more important than the person.

Managers, supervisors, coaches, and leaders are faced with situations just like the one described above every day. You simply find yourself in a very difficult spot sometimes, places you did not ask nor wish to be. It happens. And you realize that you have a decision to make. You also know it is best to step back and consider all of your options, because every option has its own set of consequences. Many times this is a very difficult task; having our full thinking mind available to us is challenging enough when we have time on our side and there are no emotions attached to our thinking. When we factor in the tension and complexity that time pressures and emotional intricacy brings, however, our task of making a good decision becomes logarithmically more difficult.

So how can we be *in the moment* with Susan? How can we suppress the very real needs we have to be in charge or to look good to our customers? Which tools do you, as a leader, possess to pull out of your tool belt in such a time as this?

Inside these pages you will learn how the blending of tools can take your management and leadership skills to a new and higher level. We will blend coaching skills with the emerging science of emotional intelligence, and the results may surprise you!

Core Values

Clarence Francis, CEO of General Foods from 1935-43, said this: "You can buy a person's time. You can buy their physical presence. You can even buy their skilled muscular motions per hour. But you cannot buy loyalty. You cannot buy enthusiasm. You cannot buy the devotion of hearts, minds and souls. These, you must EARN."

Many supervisors, managers and executives these days espouse an attitude that might better be characterized like this: "I'm paying you a certain amount per hour, so I should get a certain level of performance out of you." It is true that you can buy that. What you cannot buy, however, are loyalty and commitment from those same employees when times get tough in your organization. What reason have you given your people to stay with you when per-formance drops off or times get tough? What would make your staff want to show up for work each day when mar-ket share plummets and the bonuses temporarily dry up?

My friend, Tom, considered himself a compassionate per-son. He considers compassion to be a core value. Over the years, his faith has taught him the importance of this quali-ty. But here's how Tom characterized what he learned about compassion as a result of his situation with Susan: "The true measure of compassion is what happens at a time when it's completely unexpected. In the midst of tumult, in the midst of a job that was squeezing me to push, I was being measured on how much of that stuff we could get into a delivery truck by the end of the day. That's how we made our money and so, my whole job was dependent upon that. That really defined me."

Tom's observation represents the norm. Leaders are *not* typically measured on how compassionate they are with their employees. In fact, some organizations have begun to notice a correlation between how a leader treats an employee and that employee's productivity. Most of this awareness, however, is relegated to an annual performance review with little to no impact on the overall results of the leader (unless, of course, the behavior of the leader is so poor that it affects everyone in the organization). Yet, how did a *lack* of compassion work out for Tom? Susan took off another two weeks from work immediately following her exchange with Tom. Guess who was stuck doing his job *and* her job for yet another ten work days? In the years since then, Tom has come to realize that, had he been a little more compassionate and a little less dismissive of Susan, the outcome very well may have been different. When Susan returned to work two weeks later, Tom found her to be cold and distant toward him. When she had needed someone to care, someone to listen, someone to calm her fears, she had received none of it. She had been "ordered" back to her desk.

How might this situation have been handled differently? Well, here's what Tom came to understand: "I learned something about myself that day. Sure, I was being measured by how much work I put out the door. Yet, had I shown a little concern for Susan that day, it is very possible that more work would have been accomplished in the long run. I missed an opportunity to show Susan that she was valued, that she was connected to what we were trying to accomplish."

And the entire fiasco started with a single notion inside Tom's head: *Why won't she just do what I tell her to do?*

Let's turn this around and take a look at the scenario

from Susan's perspective. What does an employee think when this type of situation plays out for them? Here are some reactions, most of them rarely uttered out loud:

I don't respect you. Why would I give extra effort to somebody I don't respect?

I don't want to follow you.

Are you going to go through the trenches for me?

Are you going to fight for me?

Do you really understand what it is you want? You don't understand my perspective of how difficult it is to do the thing that you are asking me to do!

The real problem here isn't so much that work isn't going to make it out the door on time. The bigger challenge is a culture problem, a failure to create a coaching climate that includes trust, commitment, passion, innovation…and one that includes vision. In reality, corporate culture tends to pay lip service to things like this. We're left with a huge disconnect, one that leads to unnecessary turnover, high employee discontent and lowered productivity. What most supervisors miss in these situations is critical. In the midst of their own frustration, they lose sight of the fact that their teammate isn't feeling valued. And during that ten or fifteen minutes of lost productivity, *the employee wasn't going to be working anyway!*

On the other hand, had that employee been given a few minutes of time by the supervisor to decompress about whatever was bothering them, perhaps that same employee could have given thirty minutes of productivity capacity in fifteen minutes! How can this happen? Because that individual has been heard and comes to understand that they are valued.

Core values are ideals that guide one's choices, actions or behaviors. They represent what is *really* important to you, rather than what you *say* is important to you. Think of it as principle over preference. Core values often include traits like respect for self and others, integrity, honesty, honoring commitments, empowerment, vision and passion. Incorporating traits like these are central to your success as a coach. In a later chapter, we will take a look at what needs to happen in order to create the kind of culture that can significantly improve each of these challenges in the workplace. Coaching skills are important tools that anyone in a leadership position very much needs to possess. Whether you are coaching your 8-year-old daughter's soccer team or leading a team of senior vice-presidents, assisting others to obtain an outcome that is positive for you, for them and for the organization should always be the goal.

But if it was only that easy, I hear you say. Even if you were not as abrupt as Tom, from our earlier example, or if you implemented some good coaching techniques by really listening to Susan, you still have a problem. You still have an irate customer on the other side of the conversation with Susan. The fact is that the conversation took time, and the production deadline was missed. You did a great job for your employee, but now your most valuable asset, your customer *(remember your mission statement)*, is ticked off! Another emotional event now is yours with which to deal.

Somewhere about now you are thinking, *Why did I even take this manager job to begin with? I would have been much better off just being a graphic designer, shooting photos of bowls of fruit and getting off work on time. Instead, here I sit in a no-win situation, knowing that my 8:00am meeting with the boss will center on why our customer angrily called him at home last night.*

My 20-plus years of experience in management and leadership development have taught me a couple of things. First, coaching is a critical management tool. Leaders *will not* be successful without it. It's just that simple. If your definition of leadership sounds anything like, "one who has power, is in charge or has influence," then understand here and now that you are going to need some additional skills in working with other people. Coaching is all about improving management, leadership and the influencing of others.

Typically, the part of the equation that is routinely overlooked is the consideration for the person on the receiving end of the coaching process. Coachees have a rational and an emotional component to their being as well. So often as leaders we step back from an event, like the one described above, and say to ourselves, ...*Well, I coached them. Now the results are up to them.* This seems disingenuous, irrational and unemotional. For coaches and leaders to step away from the emotional side of business and expect rational behavior, knowing that emotions have such a strong impact on a person's ability to be rational, simply reflects poor leadership.

This point about rational decisions and emotionality is well illustrated in the 1966 Star Trek program, created by Gene Roddenberry. The show starred William Shatner as Captain James T. Kirk and each week told the tale of the crew of the starship Enterprise, beginning each episode with a narrative about the crew's five-year mission *"to boldly go where no man has gone before."* Kirk is the fiery and emotional starship captain who leads his crew of voyagers in their exploration of "new life and new civilizations." What a great metaphor for business! Kirk's frequent emotional outbursts often interfered with his decision-making. Sometimes, it blinded Kirk from seeing all of the options available to him. In such cases, he would then rely on First Officer Mr. Spock, the non-emotional Vulcan who logically stated the options at hand as well as represented the most rational course of action.

If only we had employee rosters that consisted solely of Mr. Spocks! As leaders, we wouldn't have to deal with those messy emotions; instead, we could focus solely upon implementation. Unfortunately, however, this is not the case, is it? Those we coach bring along *all* of their emotions and experiences when they arrive at work each day. The truth is, these emotions are a vital part of how we as humans have been created, so they must have some value to our work outcomes.

Our role as leaders and coaches of high performance is to

capture the essence of all the value that our people bring to the team and workplace. Through improving our coaching skills and integrating them with our own emotional intelligence, we can create better and more productive outcomes for virtually everyone in our organizations.

My goal is to help you increase your effectiveness as a coach and as a leader. Using the seven secrets contained within the pages of this book, you will begin mastering skills and techniques that will enhance your leadership in ways you may not be able to imagine. We will begin this journey together with a discussion in the next chapter on coaching models.

TWO

Building a Foundation for Coaching

The goal of this chapter is simple: identify a common language with which we are able to dialogue about coaching. So many times we assume that the other person with whom we are communicating knows precisely what we mean. Rarely is this actually the case. This chapter is an attempt to give framework and definition to coaching so we can learn what the great coaches do later in the book.

So what is coaching? The word conjures up many different meanings and connotations among different people. Here are just a few examples:

1. The International Coach Federation (ICF) says that personal and business coaching is an ongoing professional relationship that helps people produce extraordinary results in their lives, careers, business, or organizations.

2. Dr. Timothy Gallwey, a Harvard educationalist, talks about coaching as unlocking a person's potential to maximize his or her own performance. Coaching isn't teaching him or her; rather it is helping him or her to learn.

3. Ferdinand Fournies, in *Coaching for Improved Work Performance*, says that the primary purpose of coaching is to redirect a subordinate's behavior to solve a performance problem. Simply put, he says that coaching is designed to get the subordinate to stop doing what he shouldn't be doing or to start doing what he should be doing.

4. James Flaherty, in *Coaching: Evoking Excellence in Others*, suggests that the products of coaching are: a) meeting the high objective standards of the discipline in which coaching is occurring and b) understanding the other person's structure of interpretation, then in partnership alter this structure so that resulting actions effect the intended outcome.

5. A common definition often characterizes a coach as one who supports people (clients) to achieve their goals through goal setting, encouragement and questions. Unlike a mentor or counselor, a coach rarely offers advice. Coaching does not include a given solution, but should energize the coachee to solve the problem.

6. At IntegrateEI, in our *High Impact Coaching Model*, we view coaching as an active process that focuses on connecting with individuals in ways that will change behavior, enhance skills and move to action, with the ultimate goal of achieving personal, professional, and organizational goals.

Stop here for just a moment to think about how you would define coaching. Write your definition in the space below:

_____

_____

_____

_____

Perhaps for me, the best illustration of coaching takes place in Charles Perrault's story of *Cinderella*. Undoubtedly, you are familiar with this classic story in which a young girl from a rich family is deprived of her rightful station in life through some tragic misfortunes. She finds herself in a place where she does not want to be, in a house with her ugly and mean stepsisters. Destined for a role in domestic servitude, Cinderella is forced to keep up with endless menial chores and carry the responsibilities of others. The poor girl has a brutally difficult time trying to keep up with it all, not to mention endeavoring to meet the priorities of far too many bosses.

Cinderella's goal, however, is to attend the royal ball in the palace where her Prince Charming resides. It is there where she will find happiness, fulfillment and contentment. But, alas, however is Cinderella to get from the state in which she presently finds herself to that place where she wants to be? She just doesn't seem able to get there alone.

In this metaphor, Cinderella represents many of the people who would benefit from coaching. People, not unlike our young lass, feel stuck or trapped in places they don't wish to be. Many such people may even find themselves involved with others who don't treat them with dignity or respect. Yet, like Cinderella, they have no idea how to get to the proverbial ball.

The royal ball in this metaphor represents a goal, the desire to achieve. For so many of us, the goal seems so far off, even unachievable. How rewarding it would be to achieve such a high goal, yet the odds seem insurmountable.

Unlike what so often happens in life, our illustration of the popular children's story finds Cinderella meeting her goal of attending the ball. There, her dreams are ultimately fulfilled. The key question in all of this is: How does Cinderella get to the ball? Via a coach, of course!

Indeed, it is the coach that is Cinderella's transport. Her coach becomes her catalyst for change. The coach knows where she is at in her current state and is able to transport her to where she wants to be. The coach's role is to help the coachee understand where he or she is by invoking the skills and knowledge that the coachee already possesses in order to solve his or her own problems. This results in the coachee transporting himself or herself to the place that represents the achieved goal.

This metaphor for coaching is exactly what an effective coach should do. Coaches actively assist others who are seeking change or clarity. Coaches work to understand others' current conditions and then help transport them to those places where they will feel more alive and fulfilled. Sometimes the outcomes are simply traditional, reflected by situations in which the coachee just needs support and feedback on a current issue. Other outcomes may involve transformational change, like a new career or discovering an unrealized talent. Whichever the case, the coach is the vehicle that transports the coachee in achieving the desired life change.

Coaching Types

Just as there are many definitions for coaching, there are also many different types of coaching as well. Some of the broader categories of coaching are listed below:

Individual or Life Coaching: Clients are assisted in prioritizing current life needs and in looking for ways to address changes that the coachee views as beneficial.

Team Coaching: Focuses on improving the performance of a group.

Organizational Coaching: Interactions are designed for individuals or teams to improve knowledge or skill. This approach typically reflects Life Coaching or Team Coaching within the structure of an organization.

Executive Coaching: Focuses on top-level executives to effect maximum efficiencies from organizational strategies. Such strategies may include on boarding, transitioning or organizational change of most any kind. The executive also may be seeking a new skill set or simply some unbiased feedback.

Systemic Coaching: Focuses on improving the effectiveness or survival of human systems like couples, families, teams, communities. Coaching in this area requires working with both individuals and groups, setting mutually beneficial goals for each.

Ontological Coaching: This type of coaching represents a hybrid, formed by blending skills from life and executive coaching. Ontological coaching was developed by Julio Olalla, in collaboration with Rafael Echeverria and Fernando Flores. This type of coaching focuses on altering and expanding worldview in order to effect new action that better aligns with beliefs and values. Under the premise that our habits of seeing and acting serve to limit what is possible in our lives both personally and professionally, ontological coaching is an integration of *traditional* coaching (supporting others to achieve goals) with *transformational* coaching (expanding one's worldview to facilitate innovation).

How does coaching differ from other familiar business tools?

We view coaching primarily as a leadership tool. Typically, therefore, coaching isn't particularly useful as an objective end. It is a means from which a desired outcome may be obtained. As with sporting events, it is the players who participate and make on-field decisions that determine the successful and unsuccessful outcomes. Experience has shown that coaching is often confused with many of these other popular ideals:

Managing: Balancing control and direction of resources and processes. This presumes that the person serving in the role of coach is the expert and is responsible for overall outcome. This approach is often viewed as needing to tell others what to do.

Counseling: A supportive process used to help people work

through personal problems. Counseling is about insight and uncovering with a focus on solving problems involved in a patient's character traits, character style, and ways of thinking or behaving.

Behavior Modeling: Requires that demonstration of appropriate behavior takes place. While this may be appropriate in some coaching situations, a coach should never be expected to model every behavior needed for success in a given role.

Training: Used to address lack of knowledge or skill. Coaching is the best way to follow up on any training, in order to account for any return on investment expected from training efforts.

Mentoring: Supporter and encourager of protégé's personal and professional development. Mentoring provides guidance surrounding needed behaviors, emphasizes important values, and helps link to available networks. Often, mentors serve as sounding boards for ideas and feelings.

To summarize, coaching is an emotional event where relationship is paramount. Coaching can occur in many ways and with many different types of relationships.

Coaching Relationships

Supervisor to Subordinate
Peer to Peer
Employer to Employee
Friend to Friend
Customer to Vendor
Wife to Husband
Teacher to Student
Professional Coach to Coachee
Parent to Child

In the above table, the first of each pair of named relationships is designed to illustrate the one who would seem to
have the positional power within the relationship. In reality,
coaching can certainly occur in both directions.
Subordinates can and should, at times, coach supervisors.
Children can and do, occasionally, coach parents. Recently, I
was sitting at the computer with my sixteen-year-old
daughter and received some great coaching around how to
use *Facebook*, the communication and networking tool that
today's kids use to stay in constant touch with their world.

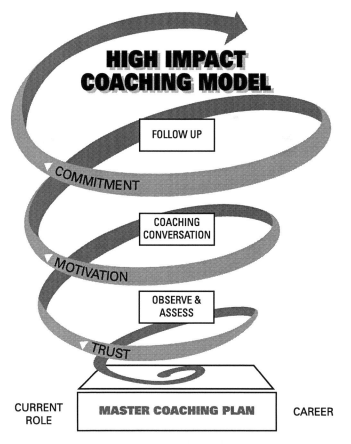

HIGH IMPACT
COACHING MODEL

FOLLOW UP

COMMITMENT

COACHING
CONVERSATION

MOTIVATION

OBSERVE &
ASSESS

TRUST

CURRENT
ROLE

MASTER COACHING PLAN

CAREER

It is with some trepidation that I put a coaching model in
this book. After all of the frustration that coaching models

have given me over the years and the realization that it is not about the boxes or ink but the people they represent, I realized that some of my readers may not have ever seen a coaching model before. If this is you, then enjoy and feel free to use this model in your inaugural journey. If you are a seasoned coach and have a different model you use, or one you like better, that is fine. I am not going to waste much more ink debating correct models. For me, coaching is about the personal interaction. I am interested in what great coaches do, which is what the remaining chapters will be dedicated to.

Coaching at IntegrateEI is an active process that focuses on connecting with individuals in ways that will change behavior, enhance skills and move to action, with the ultimate goal of achieving personal, professional, and organizational goals. Let's break down this definition into its component parts:

An Active Process: The High Impact coaching model clearly shows this activity. Sometimes you will find yourself in a simple coaching scenario where only one coaching conversation will happen (such as a demonstration of how to put gasoline in a car). If so, then this requires merely one iteration around the model. If, however, you are in a profound coaching scenario (such as career planning), then you will make several revolutions around the model over a period of time. The dynamic itself does not change. To complete the coaching process, you must stay active in traveling around the model.

Focus on Connecting with Individuals: This component formally introduces the relevance of emotional intelligence (EI) to our subject matter. EI contains within it a very important relational component. Most of the EI models you will see include a self-awareness element to them. This coaching model links the self-awareness factor to seven attributes that *emotionally intelligent* coaches possess.

Change Behavior, Enhance Skill, Move to Action: Coaching

necessitates taking the coachee to some place other than where he or she happens to be at that time. The coach must challenge the coachee with a definite call to action. Without such a call, nothing will ever happen.

Coachee Achieves Personal, Professional, and Organizational Goals: The goals of the person being coached are what this entire process revolves around. As a coach, however, you have goals also, as does your organization (or family, business, or ministry). In order for true coaching to occur, the goals that you bring to the table as a coach *must* integrate into positive benefits for the person being coached. If the coachee doesn't agree with where you are taking him or her as the coach, the risk is high that the entire process may become unraveled when the coachee ends up with "buyer's remorse."

Buyer's remorse is an emotional state whereby a person feels regret after acquiring ownership of an item. Often, buyer's remorse is linked to the purchase of higher dollar objects such as cars, boats, houses, etc. The regret typically is brought on by an inner sense of uncertainty that the correct decision was made in transacting the purchase. The concept of buyer's remorse is not limited to material possessions, however. It also can extend to the acquisition of an ideology, belief, or even a change in behavior. In the case of our example, the high value item is the person we are coaching and the behaviors he or she owns are changing with the help of a coach. In order to prevent this emotional condition where the coachee may have second thoughts and wish to *"return"* the coaching you have given, it's important to make certain that no internal sense of doubt exists for the coachee. Removing doubt requires ensuring that the person being coached has a say in whether or not the correct decision has been made relative to his or her course of action or behavior change. If the coachee agrees with the coaching, then the process can move forward to effect a hopeful and positive change.

The High Impact Coaching Model has three very distinct components. First, you will notice that the model sits upon a planning base. No coaching should occur without some kind of foundational plan. Of course, such a plan can be dynamic and may well change over time. Whether you are meeting your coachee for the very first time or you have had a relationship for a very long time, a plan is vital to maintain the continuity and direction of your coaching efforts. One important aspect of this planning function is to document coaching progress. In order to assist you with this, we have developed a coaching worksheet (below) for you to implement in your coaching work. As we work our way through the coaching model, you will be able to follow along by writing in and documenting an actual coaching situation in which you may be presently engaged.

The second thing to notice about this model is that there are three items in boxes and three items in arrows. The items inside the boxes refer to process steps that coaches take. Inside the arrows are essentials for the coachee that enable the coach to keep the process moving forward. These represent the foundation for the relationship.

Foundations are basic building blocks of structures. In the construction of homes, for example, the foundation is dug deep in the ground and supports the visual part of the building.

Foundations make the building stronger. Trust, motivation, and commitment are all integral parts of the coaching relationship. These foundational aspects of coaching exist to some extent before we ever have a relationship with the person we are coaching. These foundational aspects of coaching will continue to exist during the coaching. And they will be present at the end of the coaching. The question becomes: are people stronger or weaker as a result of our coaching? Experience shows that the more trust, motivation and commitment that can be built, the more pleased the coachee will be with the outcome. To the contrary, coaching efforts simply would not occur without them. This is the "Why won't they just do what I tell them to do?" frustration we talked about in chapter one. Futility awaits the coach who tries to advance a coaching conversation with a coachee when little or no trust exists between the two people.

In reviewing this model with one of the great coaches we interviewed, he shared the following real life experience:

"As the company's new sales manager, I had a proven performer on my team. I came into the job very much needing to show my positional power, so I began telling this person how he should be doing his job. Needless to say, the individual's performance decreased due to my coaching. *What* I was coaching wasn't the problem. Instead, it was how I was going about the coaching process. Our relationship was new. I had no credibility as a coach or leader. I only held positional power. Rather than recognizing this and building trust with this top performer, I blew it! Unaware of my lack of self awareness, I simply was not being authentic in my communication."

Have you ever found yourself in a similar situation? Reflect back over your coaching career. Consider the experiences about which today you can say, *"I really blew it in that situation and here's why."* Humbling, isn't it, to think about those times when our intentions were noble and yet we blew it?

To help you build skill in using the High Impact Coaching Model, you will find a Coaching Planning Worksheet below. This tool is designed to enable you to step back and to consider each step in the coaching model. It may be useful to you to practice using this model. In the remaining pages of this chapter, we will briefly walk through the coaching model to further illustrate how it can enhance your coaching efforts. As you walk through each step of the model, take time to come back to the worksheet and write your thoughts around someone you are coaching. This activity will take an otherwise theoretical coaching model and turn it into a useful and practical coaching tool.

High Impact Coaching Model Worksheet

1. *Master Coaching Plan*	
2. *Observe and Assess*	
3. *Trust*	
4. *Coaching Conversation*	
5. *Motivation*	
6. *Follow up*	
7. *Commitment*	

Using the High Impact Coaching Model

Begin by answering a series of questions that will greatly enable you as the coach to build a plan that impacts your coachee. What is it that is important to coach? Why is it important to coach? What are the emotional components that great coaches consider before engaging the coaching experience? (We will talk more about these emotional components in the last third of the book.) After you have satisfactorily answered those questions, you will have the basic schematic necessary for creating a successful coaching plan for your client. Once created, stick to the plan. And be certain that you guard against over-coaching!

1. Master Coaching Plan
In order to jump start thinking on relevant, major themes, a master coaching plan is briefly created. Of course, this preliminary plan may be revised over time and/or specifics may be added.

This plan should answer key questions: What are the strategic areas around which your coaching will revolve? Do they center on acquisition of a technical skill, or are they perhaps related to career discussions? The importance of such a plan in coaching cannot be overstated. Have a plan and know what you are coaching.

Are you coaching someone on a technical skill or issue such as how to drive a car? Or are you coaching someone on a career issue, such as helping them define careers goals and an action plan? Career coaching is a lot like playing checkers. My father used to say, "You can't get "kinged" if you don't have a strategy to get through the maze!"

The other benefit of having created a plan for coaching is that you, the coach, know where you are going. Equally important, it clearly shows where you have been in your coaching journey. A coaching plan demarcates what ground you have covered and what ground you may need to cover in the future.

First and foremost, the coaching plan is meant to be a road map for the coachee's success. Remember, this is a *flexible* plan and is meant to be only a road map. As with road maps, many different routes will typically lead to the desired destination.

2. Observe and Assess
Once your master coaching plan is in place, you are ready to begin the process of coaching. To properly coach someone else, you must arrive at a diagnosis regarding what certain behavior(s) may mean and how the coachee might change such behavior for their own benefit. The word diagnosis is derived from the Greek words *dia* which means "by", and *gnosis* which means "knowledge." As a coach, you must pull together *all* of your knowledge and skills to help

the coachee, to help him change whatever needs to change in order to find success. This case study may be likened to that of what a physician will do when a patient contracts a particular disease. Before the physician can begin to enter into a conversation with you about what might be wrong with your body, he or she first must make some observations and assessment. The physician will then link the sum total of gleaned information, along with his or her knowledge and experience, for the purpose of providing a diagnosis. Likely, the next conversation would revolve around a consideration of treatment options. In medicine, as one example, a diagnosis has two primary components. The first is observation, the recognition of a sign or symptom. The second is assessment, comparing what has been observed with some standard that has already been set. These two steps, observation and assessment, are equally important in the coaching process.

Individuals with abnormal *symptoms* commonly consult a physician when they believe something is wrong with their body. Unfortunately, coaching doesn't often offer the same luxury. The reason for this is that it is very difficult for people to observe their own behavior. For those who are able to observe themselves, the outcome often results in an attitude like: "That is just who I am and how I operate. If they don't like it, they can get someone else." Sound familiar? As coaches, we know that attitudes should not be that way. And as coaches, our job is to be that of a mirror. As we observe particular behaviors, we are to hold them up to a coachee and ask if he or she sees what we see. If he or she doesn't see it, our job is to help him or her see it. If he or she *can* see it, our job is to help him or her find a solution. Stay with me now: it's NOT the job of the coach to solve the problem for him or her. This is called "superhero."

Solving other peoples' problems is usually reserved for any number of fictional cartoon heroes who fill comic books and grace the silver screen. I am none of those characters, and I suspect you may not be either. But coaches who conduct themselves as superheroes recognize problems that their coachees often don't recognize until it is too late. Then, the Superhero Coach swoops in at the last possible second to save the day. We coaches know better than to don a cape and go flying in for the rescue, our focus is on the fairly unglamorous job of serving in the trenches. We recognize that what really matters is helping our coachees observe and assess their own behaviors so that they can solve their own problems.

Comparing your observation to the standard you have set
Once your observation has been made and you arrive at a diagnosis, you are ready to compare what you have seen with the standard previously set. This requires that you know what you are expecting from your coachee prior to initiating the coaching scenario. This can and should be included in your coaching pre-plan. What are you expecting to see behaviorally from your coachee? What is the minimum level of performance you need to see prior to making an observation as the coach?

Caution: Among the biggest frustrations your coachee may experience with you as a coach are shifting expectations. To the best of your ability, make certain that your expectations are built on solid, proven assumptions. The less shifting that occurs in your expectations, the more credibility you will have as a coach and the clearer your coachee will be able to see the target for which he or she is shooting.

Customize the plan to the individual
After you have observed and assessed behavior, you should begin to customize your coachee's plan. At this point, you have the freedom to make any needed changes. Keep this customization thought in your mind prior to having the coaching conversation because afterwards the expectation will be set.

In order for your coachee to feel he or she can commit to the follow up of the coaching plan, he or she needs to believe that it is real and authentic. He or she needs to know it was developed with intention and with respect for his or her own personal well being. Let's face it; we all have strengths and weaknesses. The more these behavioral attributes are described, the more your coachee will feel like you really understand him or her. The more understanding that exists between the coach and the coachee, the more committed to the development the coachee will become.

A fellow coach once said to me, "My employees won't care how much I know until they know how much I care." The more committed the coachee is to following up on the plan, the more he or she will reveal his or her true self to you. If you don't care for the coachee or about his or her success, it won't matter how smart you are or how admirable others think you are. Your legacy of performance will be irrelevant to your coachee. He or she will perceive you as just another boss trying to claw his way to the top while using him or her as a stepping stone along the way.

3. Trust

Trust is the first of the foundational coaching pillars. The stronger the trusting relationship you foster with your coachee, the further and faster progress will be. Trust does not occur in a vacuum. A vacuum is a place with little or no oxygen. Bear in mind that a trusting relationship needs room to breathe. It needs the dynamics of air and space to be able to grow and mature.

One question I have learned to ask coachees in building my coaching relationship with them is how they view trust. Typically, I articulate the question in the form of a choice they must make. For example, I might ask, "Are you the kind of person who has an immediate level of trust from the outset of the relationship such that I may either lose it or gain more as time moves forward? Or do you start with no trust of people and then work toward building trust over time?"

As the reader, how would you answer these questions? Is your trust mine to lose, or do I start with none and have to build? As is usually the case in coaching, second questions are often better than first questions, so I always ask the follow up. This approach helps make certain that the coachee has the opportunity to fully explain what he or she means. Make no mistake. If you will explore this topic of trust with the person you are coaching (whether you start with none or you have all you need), you will find that trust will increase just by having the conversation.

4. Coaching Conversation

At this point in the coaching model, you have made very significant progress. Don't forget to take some time to celebrate your achievement along the way!

Your next big step: you have begun forming the coaching plan and have made and assessed an observation against the standard already set. You also have worked on building a trusting relationship. Now, it's time to enter into that coaching conversation.

Entire books are dedicated to the topic of coaching conversations, books that cover topics like how to start coaching conversations, what happens if and when these go wrong, and how to wrap up conversations. The breadth of this topic is beyond the scope of this book. Allow me, however, to say just a few words about important elements to keep in mind as you have coaching conversations.

First, great coaches ask great questions. Great coaches ask very concise and "to the point" questions. Often, such questions are quite direct. To practice this skill in coaching, challenge yourself to use no more than seven words when asking any question to a coachee. In my experience, I have observed that most coaches and leaders like to ask complex questions *to show how smart they are.* Whether we realize it or not, we talk at length, often just to hear ourselves pontificate. We will often ask questions on top of questions, to the point where our recipient hasn't a clue what to answer or where to begin.

Here are rules that will serve you well: one short question at a time. No more than seven words in the question. Questions must be direct and to the point. Examples of this: *"Tell me about that customer"* or *"Say more about that."*

Secondly, great coaches are great listeners. We'll elaborate on this in detail in the upcoming chapter on communication. For now, however, the point is that we must listen for meaning. As a coach, it is critical that you stay curious in your listening to really try to understand the meaning behind what your coachee is telling you. Resist the temptation to judge him or her too quickly. Ask good, intentional, follow up questions as a way to stay engaged with your coachee.

5. *Motivation*
The next foundational pillar in coaching for an improved outcome is to make certain the coachee is motivated to the change he or she sees. Without sufficient motivation, the behavior change *will not happen.* Motivation comes from within the human spirit. It has very little to do with agreeing to do something verbally or in writing. For any one of us, without fully discovering the benefit of the coaching, we won't change our behaviors or our performance. So as a coach, be ever mindful of the perspective of the coachee: "What's in it for me?" What is the reward or recognition that your coachee will receive? How will he or she become better by following the plan you are laying out?

In order to advance to the next step in the model, monitoring your coachee's progress in the area of motivation is key.

6. *Follow up*
We've come to the point where most coaches fail. Coaches often fail both their clients and their employees. Here's the thought process that leads to these failures: *I have done a good job of pre-planning. I have accurately observed and assessed a behavior and compared this to a clear standard. We have had wonderful coaching conversations filled with trust and concise questioning. I have listened at least 50% more that I have talked. The coachee clearly reiterated the benefit of the coaching plan we put in place. He or she is energized and motivated to get started, knowing full well the coaching is in his or her best interest as a*

human being. At this point, many coaches slap their hands together and say job well done! *Wrong!* The job has only just started!

Key question: How will you know you are successful as a coach if you do not follow up? You need some method for measurement in order to ensure your success. Is the person *actually* implementing the behavior change? Are you seeing performance improvements?

Your coachee will need much support along the way. As part of the follow-up process, your coachee needs your encouragement. Your coachee needs to hear you say things *over and over* to reinforce everything that was accomplished in your work together. This follow-up component of the High Impact Coaching Model requires much patience. Ignore this at your peril!

7. *Commitment*

Commitment requires discipline to stick to the plan until the coachee is achieving the desired performance. Always, it's much easier to fall back into poor habits than to forge ahead with new ones, even when the new ones are better for us and yield better results.

Commitment means you will help your coachee endure *all* of the process, not just the first half. Commitment also means that the coachee has accepted and bought in to the process. As an example, you may ask a coachee to notice an undesirable behavior. In pointing this out to him or her, you may suggest that he or she reflect for five minutes at the end of each day to see if he or she remembers actually doing the behavior in question. Then, ask him or her to write this down in a notepad so that you both may talk about his or her discovery the next time you meet.

This sounds reasonable, doesn't it? You have made an observation compared to standard. You have built trust along the way. You have demonstrated that you have your coachee's best interest in mind. You have had the coaching conversation, during which he or she seemed perfectly motivated. You even follow-up to see if he or she is making progress and he or she assures you that he or she is. Then comes time to review his or her observations with him or her, and you hear something like: "I don't have the notepad with me," or "My dog ate my notepad," or "My notepad is private, I don't think I should share it," and maybe even, "Notepad, what notepad, you didn't ask me to keep notes…did you?"

Which of these do you think you are most likely to hear? As a professional coach I have heard them all *(Ok, not the one about the dog)*. At times, our coachees will seem like they are completely engaged in the coaching model only to show virtually no commitment at the end.

This is where emotional intelligence becomes instrumental in your coaching. EI is about connecting, building trust, gaining motivation and commitment for and from those we are coaching.

Hopefully, you are ready to take your coaching skills from ink and paper, and boxes and arrows, to a whole new level of performance. Implementing emotional intelligence in coaching begins with an understanding of a small area in your brain. *Are you ready to meet your amygdala?*

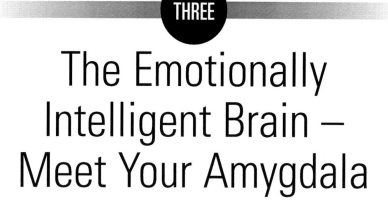

THREE

The Emotionally Intelligent Brain – Meet Your Amygdala

What separates great performers from all the rest? What separates great business people from all the others? Where does our competitive advantage lie? In this chapter, we will frame our discussion around three different dimensions that make up our being, our character.

The first dimension is intelligence quotient, commonly referred to as IQ. Typically, we refer to IQ when we talk about how smart someone is. IQ refers to the mental processes that take place between our ears.

The second dimension involves technical proficiency. If you are an accountant, how capable are you with the accounting software, or in figuring out discrepancies with numbers? If you are a radiological laboratory technician, for example, how well do you align the x-ray machine with your patients? Clearly, technical skills are very important; we measure our abilities to master them with a device called education. Technical skill is a function of our IQ, applied to skill proficiency.

IQ vs. Technical Skill vs. EI

The third dimension that is used to define a great performer is emotional intelligence, also known as EI. Likely, you may not be as familiar with EI as you are with IQ or technical skill. If that's the case, by the time you get to the end of this book, you will know quite a bit about EI! Emotional intelligence is all about the ability to connect and to communicate. So, we work with people to define star performance in all three of the aforementioned categories.

Now, take a moment and think of the name of a great leader in your life. Consider the qualities that make that person great. Probably you can think of several. Jot them down on a piece of paper, if you'd like. Now consider those qualities that you wrote down. I would guess that, just maybe, you wrote something like *vision* and maybe an *infectious smile*. Did you write risk taker? Empathy? Strong beliefs? Maybe you said something about your leader's ability to communicate.

If my guesses are correct, the attributes you used to characterize a great leader weren't technical skills or qualities that we measure with IQ. More likely, they were traits that we associate with emotional intelligence, or EI!

By itself, IQ is not a very good predictor of job performance. Researchers Hunter and Hunter estimate that, at best, IQ accounts for about 25 percent of the performance variance. Sternberg contributes to this discussion by pointing out that studies vary, and that 10 percent may be a more realistic estimate. In some studies, IQ accounts for as little as four percent of the variance. Another source that points to this phenomenon is a study of 80 Ph.D.s in the field of science who had been Berkeley graduate students in the 1950s. Back then, these 80 individuals had been part of a larger group that completed a battery of personality tests, IQ tests, and interviews. Forty years later, when they were in their early seventies, the test subjects were tracked down. Assessments of their success in life were completed on the basis of resumes, evaluations by experts in their own fields, and sources like American Men and Women of Science. The results demonstrated that social and emotional abilities were four times more important than IQ in determining professional success and prestige.

As a result of this type of work, it has been proposed that technical skills and IQ be viewed more as "threshold competencies." In and of themselves, these threshold competencies do not guarantee success in life or in careers. Instead, emotional intelligence serves as a far stronger and more reliable predictor of success.

Another classic example of the power of EI and the limits of IQ as a predictor of success is the Sommerville study. This was a 40-year longitudinal investigation of 450 boys who grew up in Sommerville, Massachusetts. Sixty-six percent of the boys were from welfare families, and the remaining third possessed IQs below 90. However, in studying the boys' IQs, the results concluded that their scores bore little relation to how well they did at work or in the rest of their lives. Instead, what made the biggest difference was mastery of childhood abilities, such as being able to handle frustration, control emotions, and get along with other people.

An example of the practical impact of emotional intelligence upon success and performance is reported by Goleman, Boyatzis and McKee in their classic book on emotional intelligence and leadership, *Primal Leadership*. A study of partners at a large public accounting firm showed that those with significant strengths in self-management contributed 78 percent more incremental profit than partners who did not possess the same skills. Additionally, partners with strong social skills added 110 percent more profit than those with only self-management competencies. This resulted in a 390 percent incremental profit annually. Interestingly, those partners with significant analytical reasoning skills contributed only 50 percent more incremental profit.

Let's more closely examine this thing called emotional intelligence. Simply put, EI is the ability to manage one's emotions and the emotions of others. Researchers Salovey and Mayer first coined the term emotional intelligence in

1990, aware of the previous work on noncognitive aspects of intelligence. They described emotional intelligence as "a form of social intelligence that involves the ability to monitor one's own and others' feelings and emotions, to discriminate among them, and to use this information to guide one's thinking and action." In 1995, science writer Dan Goleman picked up on the work of Salovey and Mayer, and he published his first book on this subject, entitled *Emotional Intelligence*. In his research, Goleman linked the research of Salovey and Mayer to that of the work of New York University's Joseph LeDoux, an early researcher in the field of neuropsychology. Today, Goleman is considered to be the authoritative voice in the field of emotional intelligence, having published a number of books on the topic.

In practice then, if EI is characterized as managing one's own self and others' emotions, then what types of roles does emotional intelligence play in business settings? Practically speaking as coaches, EI becomes relevant in how we manage our emotions during those times when we are with a client and the client just happens to be boring us to death. EI becomes the key difference maker in moving difficult situations forward or backward. How can we manage ourselves to stay in the moment, to really focus on the client and not on ourselves?

A key aspect of emotional intelligence is doing what we have to do to be able to manage a tough situation for a better outcome. The issue may not always revolve around how emotions negatively impact us, but rather how we manage emotions rather than control them. We tried controlling them, right? Remember "management by objective?" Let's see, what was the mantra? "Set your goals. Check your emotions at the door. Then pick up your emotions on the way out the door, but don't dare bring them into the workplace." Sound familiar? Didn't work very well, did it?

So, how much does emotional intelligence really impact the workplace? The truth is that EI has a huge impact up and down the corporate ladder, from the people on the line who spend the day on repetitive tasks all the way up to the executives in the boardroom. Recognizing the role that emotion plays in the workplace means the wise supervisor or coach can help produce better outcomes. In a study on leadership called "Emotional Competence and Leadership Excellence" (Johnson & Johnson), the impact that emotions play on performance was again confirmed. In a study of 358 managers, the results showed that the highest performing managers possess significantly more "emotional competence" than do other managers.

Emotional intelligence skills and efficiencies, therefore, are essential ingredients for any professional who coaches others in the workplace. Integrating emotion and intelligence into the skills and talents that your organization's people possess leads to entirely new levels of achievement and success.

An executive with whom I work is responsible for coaching his subordinates. Recently, he said to me, "Scott, they bore me. The pettiness they bring to the job bores me." My response was to remind him that he wasn't going to get much done in his organization without them. Instead, I advised him to really tune in to them, to focus on what they really meant beyond the words they expressed. Abraham Lincoln once made the statement: *"I don't like that man very much... I'm going to have to get to know him better."*

We are emotional beings with real feelings that drive our behaviors. This is true for our clients. It is true for our employees. And it's true for us. So when we talk about leadership, we must consider emotion and how it impacts and drives performance.

Think this doesn't really matter in your office? Marcus Buckingham, in his best seller, *First Break All The Rules*, writes that many major companies now lose and replace about half of their customers every five years. A very good friend of mine recently related to me just how much time and effort he observes the typical company investing on securing new customers, in an effort to try to make up for the many that they are losing. The same is true for employees. Employee turnover is very costly, and yet we know that, more often than not, people leave supervisors and not companies.

A few years ago, United Airlines ran a television commercial that featured a room filled with executives. The boss walks in and blurts out: "I just got off the phone with our oldest and biggest client. He FIRED us!!! He said, "We've lost touch with our clients." Then the boss passes out United Airlines tickets to everyone in the room so they can immediately connect with all of their customers. When asked who he was planning to visit, the boss says: "I'm going to call on that old friend who just fired us, to see if I can earn his business back." United Airlines created and ran their entire advertising campaign around the recognition that *lost* customers were important to their success. Building connection and trust with clients and employees is precisely what makes the difference. How profitable would our companies be if we just kept the customers that we had? Yet, how much time and effort do companies spend on retaining existing customers as opposed to seeking new ones? Emotional intelligence has everything to do with solving this age-old dilemma.

Do you understand why customers leave, why their loyalties are lost? During Markus Buckingham's years working with the Gallup organization, he discovered a direct correlation between how engaged employees are with clients to client loyalty. Likely, you've noticed that in your own business, even intuitively. The source of customer loyalty is your customer's feeling that you care about him or her.

By the same token, what causes an employee to be engaged? Buckingham suggests that this comes through the direct supervisor relationship. Everything rises and falls on how well-connected employees feel to their supervisors. Do your firm's supervisors, in fact, have your employees' best interests in mind? Can you cite the number one reason that people leave their company? You may be surprised to learn that it's not about compensation. It's not even about upward mobility. People leave companies because of their direct supervisors, because they don't feel valued or connected. How much more successful could a company be if it simply recognized and changed this dynamic?

So, as coaches (and it is assumed that we are a reasonably intelligent lot), why do we fail? What are some of the reasons why really smart coaches find their bright futures and shining careers derailed? The Center for Creative Leadership discovered two traits that often represent the root causes of such failures: an inability to manage relationships and an inability to manage change. Let's take a look at what precipitates these two insidious enemies of success.

Brain Science 101

The secret is that there is biology (yes, science) behind this whole emotional intelligence dynamic. Having had the benefit of a science background, I rather enjoy using some of my training in this area. Let's break this down into some simple components.

The brain is a very complex organ. The brain's ultimate power is derived from the intricacies that it possesses. Likely you knew that already. Researchers learn more every day about how the human brain functions. For our purposes, we will examine the brain's role in how we manage our emotions so as to be more effective and more present with those we coach. What we refer to as the brain really starts where the organ attaches itself to the spinal cord, at the very base, in a place called the brain stem. This particular location of the brain isn't terribly important for skills that require cognition like math or science. On the other hand, it is vitally important if you like your lungs to breathe and your heart to beat! The brain stem is where many of your reflexes are centered, those unconscious parts of your brain that few of us ever think about. We breathe in and we breathe out, and our heart beats without our thinking about it. It just happens. It's autonomic. It's automatic.

In the science of emotional intelligence, the next part of the brain to consider is called the amygdala. This is the region of the brain that NYU's LeDoux has researched extensively. The amygdala represents your site for emotional learning and emotional memory. This is the area of the brain that allows us to learn for the first time, before we gain a lot of cognitive brain components. The amygdala is also the place where we store emotional memory. Interestingly, the amygdala was actually featured on one episode of the popular medical forensic television show, *CSI*. The characters in the show actually discussed the amygdala and explained what happens when it is damaged. Without our amygdala and the emotions that it facilitates within us, decisions would be nearly impossible for us to make.

The amygdala is that "fight or flight" center that you've heard about. When faced with fear, our brain asks and answers the question: "Do I fight what I fear or do I run from it?" The amygdala searches our environment for fear; when we sense fear, we act or react. It's fight or flight.

Another region of the brain in our discussion is the neocortex. This is where your intelligence resides and where all of those mental thought processes occur. All of our thinking and our entire working memory can be found here. Stated another way, this is the intelligent part of our mind, precisely where the IQ is centered.

Let's say, for example, that we are walking through a jungle and we become aware of some rustling in the nearby grass. We move toward it to take a peek. Inside the tall foliage, we observe a large snake. What do we do? We run, of course. We don't stop and think about it, right? *Snake! Bam! We're outta here!* It's all reflex. There is no time to count the snake's stripes or study its scale pattern. Those would involve cognitive or IQ brain function. We also don't observe the snake's beautiful eyes or measure the length of its tongue. Our bodies are doing one thing...preparing to protect self by either fighting or running! The amygdala says FEAR and triggers the mind to implement: fight or run.

In this case, "snake" equates to "RUN!" The amygdala actually sends a message down to the brain stem, and the brain stem then sends a little message down to two triangularly shaped things, called adrenal glands, that sit on top of the kidneys. These adrenal glands secrete what are called *stress hormones*, adrenaline and cortisol. The adrenaline increases heart rate and breathing. At such a moment, an increased heart rate and increased breathing rate are exactly what is needed! Along with that, cortisol increases blood pressure, sending blood and oxygen to the muscles. As a result, cortisol prepares the body for a fight by enabling strong muscular contraction.

You may be thinking, *Okay, what's up with the snake thing? I don't work in a jungle.* Oh really? In many of the companies with which I work, I frequently hear the environment referred to as a jungle! Does this sound remotely familiar? My boss walks down the aisle of my cubicle, and I can feel my heart rate go up. I can feel tension creeping up my neck. That's cortisol in action, being secreted into your mouth and into your neck. And cortisol just sits there until something is done to remove it. One reason I encourage those whom I coach to get into some sort of an exercise program is because they have to be able to get the cortisol out. If it doesn't get worked out of our system, it's toxic. Long-term exposure to cortisol has been shown to have detrimental effects and can even impair learning functions.

The amygdala performs another function when triggered. When it senses that fear about which we've just been talking, it shuts down the thinking in the cortex. The amygdala short-circuits your brain because it does not want you to be thinking. It just wants you to be running. Call it self-preservation! Have you ever been in a conversation with someone involving tension and complexity? When those two things come into play, you often just can't quite think of what to say, can you? Yet, once back at your desk, you mumble to yourself: "Oh! I wish I hadn't said that!" Or, more commonly, "Where was that great thought when I needed it?" Have you ever stumbled over what to say in a presentation, and then in your car a few minutes later thought: *Man, I wish I just would have said that.* It happens all the time. Here's the science at work: you've experienced what Dan Goleman (in *Emotional Intelligence*) calls an "amygdala hijack." The amygdala quite literally hijacks your thinking mind. It forces your neocortex to hold those thoughts that aren't needed at that moment, and it just screams, "REACT."

Managing Your Amygdala

The question often posed to me is, "Can I control this reaction?" Researcher LeDoux tells us that this brain function literally fires faster than we can think. His research suggests that we can feel before we can think. It's automatic. And, truth be told, it's a good thing. Right? After all, if you step off the curb at a street corner with a bus headed straight for you, you don't especially have to assess how big the bus is. Do you? You just want to get out of the way. Right? The same thing is true for the people with whom we work, as well as the clients with whom we interact.

This physiological function that occurs at the pleasure of our amygdala stops complex thoughts to such an extent that we often can't think clearly, or at all. Have you ever been sitting with a client and felt your heart rate speeding up, then your breath rate begins increasing? Physically feeling that tension and complexity brings to our attention this process that is occurring in our brain. The question is, how do we get our thinking minds back? We will explore this further in the pages ahead.

First, let's take a look at some trademarks of an amygdala hijack. Imagine that you're meeting with a person you are coaching. The coachee begins to give you some feedback on how you did not perform well a task he or she felt you as a coach should have implemented flawlessly. Suddenly, you begin experiencing a nauseating feeling in your stomach, and your breathing becomes more rapid. Soon after, you left the meeting. But you can't remember a thing that was said. This is a classic case of your body's strong emotional response, affected by your brain chemistry.

When the "amygdala hijack" is over and you regain your composure, two things can happen. Either we act out our default behavior (like retreating back onto the street corner and out of the path of an oncoming bus) and blow up (soon wishing we hadn't) or we swallow our truth and end up feeling anger, depression or any number of other negative emotions.

If an amygdala hijack sounds like something to which you can relate, the next chapter we will correlate this biology to our inspiration as coaches.

FOUR

Enhancing Coaching Success by Understanding EI

Inspiration

It is everything you think it is. It is the end of the tunnel and the light up ahead. It is the sound of the wind and the silence of the night. It is the sun and moon and the memory. It is the eye and the hand and the mouth. It is the present and the future and the past. It is here. It is there. It is gone.

Charles Ghigna, A Fury of Motion

E motional intelligence (EI) is an inspirational science for coaches. Oh yes, certainly EI is about improving and enhancing performance. Whether it's at the office or at home, emotional intelligence is about creating better outcomes by building stronger, more meaningful relationships. This is inspiring! We, as coaches, have the opportunity to dramatically impact and inspire others' lives.

Recently, I was leading a "High Impact" coaching seminar. One of the participants approached me at the break, visibly frustrated. "Scott," he said, "I have always thought I was a pretty good coach, but I must be losing it. I tell my people what to do and they just won't do it. What do you think could be going wrong?" He continued, "I attended our company's communication class and learned how to set SMART goals and give very clear instructions. My life would be easier if they would just do what I tell them to do!"

The beginning of this inspiration is understanding that, in the moment, emotion drives behavior. We *must* look to the underlying emotion at work if we are trying to improve our performance. So many times in the process of communication, we designate the *other* person as the source of difficulty. For any number of reasons, we rarely point the guilty finger at ourselves first.

Emotional intelligence starts with self-awareness. We will devote an entire chapter of this book to the subject of self-awareness, but for the sake of helping to define emotional intelligence, we come to recognize an awareness of our emotions and the impact they have on others. The good news is that once this skill is developed, we can then reach out and be more in tune with others' emotions. Being in tune with others and their emotions is a definition of empathy, another one of the seven secrets. Becoming self-aware is about knowing yourself and being confident enough in yourself that you can truly care about the other person. This is a great way to describe authenticity, another one of our secrets. Many of us have a difficult time with this, often because examining our own self means that we must be in tune with, and even like, what we see.

The ultimate in self-awareness is being comfortable enough so that we are able to love ourselves. Explained another way, emotional intelligence is about being able to love yourself and to leave your own self in order to truly understand others. But what are the skills and talents needed to be able to accomplish this? What is required to first love yourself and then love the other person you are coaching? If you have conflict within yourself or you do not know your values structure, you may well find it tough to love yourself enough to be a coach to someone else. This is what makes coaching unique from mentoring or advising.

Having an emotional connection with yourself isn't necessary in order to offer someone advice. Possessing intellectual capacity or knowledge of a process is really all that is required in doling out advice.

If someone at the office approached you, for example, and revealed that the firm's most valuable employee had been caught stealing and then asked what should be done, the easy advice would be to follow company policy and terminate the employee. A different approach would be to suggest that this person sit down with the employee to find out what was really going on before a decision is made. This "advice" may or may not be what the person had sought, but this is where coaching takes on a new dimension. Coaching helps the person seeking assistance to solve the dilemma for himself.

In order to coach someone about what needs to be done so as to be confident in his own abilities and values, he must come to see the necessity of "leaving" himself temporarily. This helps enable him to understand the other person's perspective. "Leaving oneself" is coaching. Showing concern for the person being coached is also coaching.

In order to really care about the person on the other side of your coaching relationship, you must be centered in yourself. Coaching becomes about transporting the coachee from where he or she is in the moment to where he or she wants to be in the future. This may occur in an instant or it may take some time. Your role as coach is all about guiding him or her along the journey. Such coaching takes focus, commitment, passion and caring. These qualities all relate to our values, and in order to give of ourselves, we absolutely must know ourselves. If you are secure in what your values are and how you prioritize them, I recommend an in-depth values assessment. This tool will serve to increase the confidence you have in yourself.

Coaching also empowers the person asking the questions because the questioner becomes accountable for assisting the coachee in the discovery of the desired outcome. While the coach is accountable to the person being coached, in reality, it is the coachee who is responsible for the outcome being sought.

Coaching holds another advantage over mentoring, in that, as coaches we don't have to know the right answers. In coaching, there is the potential for mutual discovery. In a mentoring relationship, advice is often sought and given. What if your advice does not fit my personality style? What if we are from different cultures? This mentoring can create conflict on one end of the relationship and disappointment on the other end. Confrontation and let down can typically be avoided in the coaching role, because coaching allows me to be me and you to be you. The coach helps the coachee discover what is true for him or herself in order to obtain the outcomes he or she desires.

Emotional intelligence has been defined by many people many different ways. Let's examine a few of them. In Dr. Steven Stein's book, *The EQ Edge*, emotional intelligence is referred to as "the soft skills that do so much to determine our success."

Dr. Reuven Bar-On suggests that emotional intelligence is a series of overlapping but distinctly different skills and attitudes. These may be grouped under general themes, such as an array of non-cognitive (emotional and social) capabilities, as well as competencies and skills that influence one's ability to succeed in coping with environmental demands and pressures.

Authors Peter Solvoy and Jack Mayer describe EI as the "ability to perceive emotions to access and generate emotions so as to assist thought, to understand emotions and emotional meanings, and to reflectively regulate emotions in ways that promote emotional and intellectual growth."

Researcher Dr. JP Pawliw-Fry portrays EI as the ability to manage our emotions and the emotions of those around us. Finally, author and sales trainer Mitch Anthony explains in his book *"Selling with Emotional Intelligence"* that the functions of the cerebral mind are to criticize, decipher, judge, negotiate, and control. He goes on to suggest that awareness, however, is a big mind function that helps us to know sense, and to accept ourselves and others. As such, this "mindfulness" function helps us to receive input from others and to respond appropriately, as well as to merge and connect with others smoothly.

Why Should EI Matter to Me?

Emotional Intelligence is vital because it is the key that unlocks the skills necessary to be a great coach. Coaching is about *communication*. To be a great communicator, you need to recognize when setbacks are occurring and then adapt to respond through coaching. This requires *adaptability* to be able to be *empathetic* with those being coached. Coaches need to be adaptable to many different circumstances that occur and then be empathetic with the person being coached during times of difficulty and change. To be able to understand someone else, a coach also must know his or her own authentic values. This level of *authenticity* leads to acute self-awareness in the moment with the coachee. These are the links that exist between the *Seven Secrets of an Emotionally Intelligent Coach*.

Therefore, coaching is about transporting. It is the vehicle or tool utilized in leadership that allows us to help others recognize where they are, and then assists them in getting to where they want to be. Let's revisit our earlier analogy to the story of Cinderella. This fairy tale also serves to paint the perfect illustration for us in describing the transport function inherent in coaching. When faced with her dilemma, how did poor Cinderella ever manage to actually get to the ball? Standing there with her fairy godmother, Cinderella needed a way to bridge the distance between where she stood and the Royal Ball. What vehicle does Cinderella have at her disposal to transport her from life controlled by her evil stepmother to the fulfillment of her position in destiny? So often, we become so focused on the destination that we miss the entire journey along the way. Yet, it's this journey that holds much of the true excitement. Here, joy and anticipation meet to reveal a bit of what the end result will be like.

And so it is the *coach* that takes on the role of the vehicle that transports us to this final destination. Cinderella's fairy godmother, who at the time was a valuable mentor, used a pumpkin to paint a self-portrait for our heroine. Suddenly, the pumpkin becomes an actual coach...the kind that takes a person from where they are now to a place where they want to be.

I am often asked by people curious about the coaching relationship, "Can't I get there by myself?" Well, sure you can! But it is often a lonely walk (especially for those at the top of organizations), filled with questions about the unknown. It is of tremendous value to be on the journey with someone who has an objective view of your best interest in mind. Like Cinderella, you may have exposure to the elements. The beating sun, the darkness of the night, or the rain pelting you along the way all serve as possible distractions to keep you from your appointed destination. Many who have seen the benefits of the coaching relationship admit to not being able to achieve the objective solely on their own.

When you're riding in the coach, your ride is more efficient because you are protected from these elements that would endeavor to stop your journey. You may still get a little wet or dirty along the way, but you will have someone there to guide you, to help you think and to help you consider your options for the best outcome. All along, the coachee is still in control of the decisions.

In order to be of real value to the coachee, the coach *must* be in tune with his own emotional intelligence. Since emotion drives behavior, it is essential to understand that which is at the root of behavioral outputs. As coaches, to be of value in transporting clients to where they want to be, we must be able to manage our emotions efficiently. If not, we will have a tough time coaching. We may be able to give advice or even *intimidate* someone with our positional power, but we won't be able to transport him or her to *his or her* destination.

Developing EI

How does one go about learning or assimilating emotional intelligence? As an example, let's use the analogy of assessing your EI like we might assess the value of our home or real estate. Each of the points below was gleaned from a government real estate acquisition web site. Following each numbered point, we will then look at how to acquire or improve EI using common real estate language. As in real estate, experts use both science and opinions to develop usable assumptions. Each of us ultimately determines where we are (or we undergo 360-degree feedback and others tell us where they see us), and then the marketplace gives us feedback on your opinion. Okay, here's the real estate acquisition analogy:

1. Notify owner of the agency's intentions to acquire the property.
   The first step in evaluating emotional intelligence is the recognition of its existence. You must acknowledge that this emotional state exists and then become aware of where you are. The best place to start is by reading about the science (we touched on this in the last chapter). The signature book on the science of EI is called *Emotional Intelligence,* authored by Daniel Goldman. There is also a very good article in Harvard Business Review called *On Becoming a Leader* (www.hbr.com). Additional quality sources on the subject include *EQ Edge,* by Stephen Stein, and *The Manager's Pocket Guide to Emotional Intelligence,* by Emily Sterrett.

2. Appraise the property and invite the owner to accompany the appraiser.
   In the world of emotional intelligence, there are many ways to appraise your situation. Self-tests are available at local bookstores for about $5. Opportunities exist online through registered examiners to complete a validated EI assessment (for example, MHS administers the BarOn 125i; more information on this is available at www.mhs.com). These exams will give you some idea of where you are within the constructs of the competencies that the aforementioned authors have described. Be advised, however, that self-assessments like these are a bit like sewing your own clothes. It will feel good for you because you did it

yourself. Your new outfit, however, may not exactly represent the latest in fashion. Self-assessment devices give results measured only from one's own perspective. A better approach to assessment compares one's own thoughts to the thoughts that others may have. Through the use a 360-degree feedback tool, perspectives from many aspects of your life (supervisors, subordinates, peers, family, clients, etc.) may be incorporated into the overall results. Such an appraisal then delivers an output much like a real estate professional conducts an appraisal when listing a home for sale.

3. Review the appraisal.
The review of an emotional intelligence assessment is best done with the counsel of a professional, just as in real estate. While certainly there are those who sell their homes by owner, in doing so they forego the advice of a skilled professional. Such experts typically make the process easier to understand so that intelligent decisions can be made. The review of one's EI feedback is no different. A professional coach, certified in emotional intelligence, is the best option for assessing this type of feedback.

4. Establish just compensation for the property.
As with real estate, you will get what you pay for in the field of emotional intelligence coaching and assessment. While it is possible to hire a coach for a one-time assessment, this is a bit like selling your property on your own. A much wiser approach would be to expect a meaningful development plan to result from your EI assessment. Doing so typically means working with a coach for six to twelve months, so as to acquire necessary behavior changes from the feedback. Working with a professional coach will carry a price tag for quality work over that period of time. Just as you generally need someone in real estate who knows the local market, do not overlook the critical importance of hiring a coach who specializes in emotional intelligence and who has experience and certification in this discipline.
5. Provide owner with written offer and summary statement for

property to be acquired.

In the end, the process should deliver a development plan that is based on one's 360-degree assessment. A qualified coach is instrumental in developing such a plan, and then assisting the coachee to stay focused on achieving the desired results.

What Should I Expect to Gain?

The benefits of developing emotional intelligence will become readily noticeable. One may certainly expect to develop significant skill in the coaching arena. Of particular interest to most who navigate the process of developing emotional intelligence is a newly acquired and intimate knowledge of oneself.

If you should decide to avail yourself of such resources, you will come to know your strengths as well as areas for development. You will become aware of any blind spots in your coaching and how you can overcome them. You will be able to better connect as a coach with your coachee. You will discover true empathy and, as a result, be able to serve as a transport for your coachee. And you will recognize those places or situations where you are vulnerable for an emotional hijack as a coach. *How valuable would it be to you to be able to have a better handle on the circumstances that foreshadow the actual temporary loss of your thinking mind?* Since EI is about helping you make better decisions and have better outcomes, being an effective coach means that you must begin with yourself before you can truly help your coachee.

Now What?

So, what comes next? Let's say that you now have developed skill as a coach. You are no longer responsible for all of the outcomes, but you do have some accountability. You truly have the power to transfer ownership of decisions to their rightful place in your organization. Herein lies the tension in the responsibility/ accountability continuum. If you are giving wrong advice or improper direction, you are both responsible and accountable. On the other hand, in the coaching role, responsibility for results shifts to the coachee. This is rather like stopping at a gas station and asking directions. The clerk at the station who is giving the directions (whether he accurately understood what you were asking or not) is responsible for the directions given, not accountable for you reaching your destination. But a coach is more of a guide. Coaches assist us through the wrong turns, guide us along the way, and encourage us when we are headed the way we want to go. They also stand ready to make suggestions when we are off course.

Coaches should often ask if the coachee wants to "turn" at a certain location, though coaches should *not* force coachees to do so. The decision and responsibility for outcomes in a coaching framework remain with the coachee, no matter what the intention. Should the coachee decide to go his own way and, by doing so, steer off course, then the coach will recalibrate his route to help him reach his destination.

This approach to coaching allows for better outcomes in leadership development than mentoring could ever hope to give. Mentoring, of course, is not wrong. Mentors certainly may take a coaching role. There are, however, distinct differences between the two skills. Because your path may have been different from mine, your experiences may have not equaled mine, so your advice may fit you well...but *not* fit me. Being emotionally intelligent allows your great coaching skills to surface while affording your coachee the flexibility to be himself and to grow within the constructs of who he has been created to be.

What's more, this process also allows you as the coach to be who you are, authentic and real. You don't have to be *all knowing*. In being real and vulnerable, you will be viewed as a true and caring leader rather than a totalitarian dictator.

EI skills allow you to truly connect with your coachee. The acquisition of emotional intelligence will allow you to understand what coachees, as individuals, really value. If you want passion, commitment, excellence, and extra effort from those around you, you must be able to connect with them. You need to be able to understand their needs, wants, and desires and then connect with these. You *can* do this. If you do, you will be able to set your coachees free to grow into the high-performing individuals they were created to be. If you do, you will gain an entirely new freedom to work on the things you are responsible for, the things you like, the things that bring you enjoyment and pleasure. This will happen because you will have left the "command and control" style of leadership behind and entered into the realm of empowering, servant leadership. Effective coaching through emotional intelligence is the key to a dramatic change that awaits you, a change that will revolutionize how you coach and how you lead.

PART II

The Seven Secrets

FIVE

The Genesis of the Seven Secrets

There is nothing quite like a nice, hot bowl of chili on a crisp, fall evening. I must say that my wife has one of the best chili recipes that I have ever tasted. Despite the fact that she has never entered her recipe in a chili cook-off, I would guarantee a victory for her if she ever decided to compete! Good friend's cold drink and spicy hot chili…there is simply nothing like it. Throw in a little college or pro football, and you really can't beat that combination.

These seven secrets of an emotionally intelligent coach came together not unlike an award-winning recipe for homemade chili. Years of experience as a coach and a developer of coaching workshops have enabled me to easily identify the basic ingredients for coaching success. The recipe starts with two people, each of who is willing to invest in enhancing the performance of a particular skill. Then, these two people require a venue at which this coaching may take place. In addition, they need the appropriate environmental temperature for the relationship to season. Occasionally, a little overindulgence in the coaching necessitates a little antacid to settle everything down.

Many people around the world have concocted their own "secret" recipe for what they think is the *best* chili. From one contest to the next, cook-off judges endlessly hear chili cooks claiming theirs is the best recipe ever put together. The difference in the final outcome, however, often depends on the quality of the ingredients that go inside the pot.

In framing our coaching model, it's important to note that any coaching model can provide structure and common language. Certainly that is the easy part. By the same token, most anyone can throw together a few ingredients and call it chili. Only after the coaching structure is in place is there an opportunity for the coaching to get *spicy*. When the human element is added, then *how* coaching is accomplished becomes more important in achieving goals than where one might be in the coaching model process.

Okay, back to the chili analogy. As we've alluded to, the difference between good chili and *great* chili is the quality of the ingredients that are placed into the soup. The search for how coaching is done by the master chefs of the world becomes our next quest. We are interested, from a coaching perspective, in what Jim Collins sets out to answer for organizations in his book, "Good to Great." What *does* separate good from great? By the same token, which distinctions routinely occur that allow us to differentiate between bad and good coaches?

The research you will read in the coming chapters revolved around better understanding the dynamics between bad, good, and great coaches. We asked the following three questions to hundreds of people in coaching workshops and seminars:

1. Think about a bad coach you have had in your life. What made them so poor?

2. Now, think about a good coach you have had in your life. What made them good?

3. Finally, think about a great coach you have had in your life. What made them so great?

Three interesting observations resulted from the responses to these questions. First, we learned that the bad coaches were seen as lacking in all three of the drivers of success: intelligence quotient (IQ), technical skill and emotional quotient (EQ). As you might imagine, this trifecta had a significant impact on differentiating bad coaches from good coaches. And not surprisingly, we discovered that when someone talked about a bad coaching experience, it was often framed as *"the coach didn't know what they were talking about."* Upon further clarification of this observation, we found a correlation between this result and a perceived lack of credibility on the part of the coach, fueled by one of two assumptions. The first assumption was the coach lacked the intelligence to be in the role in the first place. There was a fundamental inability to think at a sufficiently high level so as to solve problems in a timely manner. The other assumption was that if the coach didn't possess a fairly high IQ, then the perception was that the coach did not possess enough experience. When questioned further, many respondents revealed that they had reserved judgment to see if time would enhance the coach's success.

The research further revealed that IQ and technical skill were viewed very much as author Daniel Goleman describes "threshold competencies" for coaching. If you don't possess these traits, you may actually have more than enough EQ and yet still not succeed!

Since our research did not include any IQ testing on coaches, we are not here to say with any certainty whether or not bad coaches actually lack intelligence or simply lack experience.

The focus of this book is on emotional intelligence. As one example of how this has *everything* to do with the quality of coaching, consider this: (a) bad coaches typically lack empathy which (b) is driven from a lack of knowledge and (c) most likely the result of an insecure self.

The second observation revealed that it was assumed that both the good and the great coaches in coachees' lives were smart enough and had the technical *know how* to have the job. In both the good and great coaching groups, trust developed between the coach and the coachee, based largely around the intelligence and technical expertise of the coach. So in these two groups, the difference was not a lack of IQ or technical skill. The clear difference between a good coach and a great coach became a matter of emotional intelligence.

The final observation dealt with the differences that coachees saw in their coaches using perceived emotional intelligence to categorize them as good or great. Seven qualities (or efficiencies) emerged when people talked about the great coaches. We call these qualities *efficiencies* because they are observational on our part. Had we measured the differences, we would have termed them competencies, a term you will often hear them referred to in many other books and articles on EQ. While there is very little difference between what we are calling an efficiency and what others have called a competency, the point is that readers should understand that our research was strictly observational; further work must be done to quantify these observations for the purpose of entering the realm of competency.

One other interesting observation emerged from the research. There was a noticeable difference in the way people described the good and great coaches in their lives. When describing the good coaches, the descriptions were very *matter of fact*. Very little emotion accompanied the description and there was a tone of expectation. The surveyed assumed that because it was part of the person's role to coach, that they were adequate of skill.

When describing the *great* coaches, however, a noticeable increase in excitement and enthusiasm was evident when talking about their great coach! Nonverbal communication became readily apparent: people often sat forward, jutted their shoulders toward their head. Sometimes their eyes lit up! A certain confidence exuded from their description of the great coaches in their lives. As they talked about these influential coaches in their lives, their words came not only from their intellect but also from their heart. A feeling that could only be described as gratitude or appreciation was evident as they talked about that one special coach who had taken the time to invest in them.

The qualities we captured as interviewees shared about their great coaches became apparent as the seven secrets that comprise an emotionally intelligent coach. The pages that follow will describe these attributes in detail, so that you will understand what people are desperately seeking in a great coach. Exercises to help you improve in these areas are also provided. Do yourself a favor and don't just read through the exercises. Go ahead and actually *do* the exercises. Don't just assume you are capable or competent at something. Take the time to create the habits necessary for you to improve your coaching skills.

After all, you never know when one of your employees, peers, or children will be in one of our seminars when we ask this question about great coaches. Will they think of *you?* Will *you* be the individual that comes to mind? If coaching is one of your primary leadership tools, consider dedicating yourself to improving your skills and abilities. If you do, your teams will be able to achieve more than you ever thought possible!

SIX

Secret #1: Self-Awareness

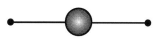

S imon never saw it coming. How did he end up in the vice president of distribution's office with the door shut? The assistant who ushered him into the office and closed the door didn't even offer him a bottle of water or a cup of coffee. "This is not going to be good," Simon thought to himself as he waited for the senior executive to come into the office.

Simon is a manager in a trucking distribution center. A technical genius in his field of distribution logistics, Simon had created many of the online tools that his firm was using to stay ahead of their competition. Simon created so much value for his organization that when a management opening occurred in his department, Simon was the logical choice for the promotion.

Since Simon's promotion created an opening in his new department, he was tasked with helping to find his replacement. Simon contacted the local community college to ask if there were any students with the requisite technical skills. The dean recommended three students, each of whom Simon interviewed. "Julie" stood out from the crowd in the interview process and so Simon hired her on the spot. She reminded Simon of himself about ten years his junior.

As the vice president strolled into the office, she started talking even before she got to her desk. "Simon, you have a problem," she declared. Stunned and dazed, Simon just sat there. The VP continued, "Since her initial training, Julie has been a very high performer, creating high value for the business. She is a whiz on the technical, logistical side of the operation…just like you, Simon. She is also very talented at working with customers."

"This isn't so bad," Simon thought to himself. "She must just really like Julie."

"You have to do something about Julie," the vice president barked. "She is creating a great deal of animosity on the floor. Can you not see it?"

Simon was not sure how he answered that question. He couldn't quite recall how it was that he had extracted himself from the executive's office. The next thing he remembered was walking back to his desk. How could he have missed Julie making everyone else in the department so upset?

Simon knew he was going to struggle in his coaching with Julie, because this was not a technical skill nor was it a knowledge gap. Instead, this was a people issue. Simon hated these! "Why won't employees just do what we ask them to do?" Simon thought to himself. Had it been a technical issue with one of the logistics programs, Simon would know exactly what to do. But, alas, Julie had all of the technical skill and knowledge she needed, yet was lacking something much more difficult to grasp: personal influence.

"The challenge for me," Simon thought to himself, "is getting Julie to recognize, believe and own this behavior in herself, and then I need to coach her on how to influence people in her own organization."

The real challenge, Simon began admitting to himself, was increasing his own self-awareness of what was going on around him, so that a meeting like that with the vice president never happened again.

The first secret of an emotionally intelligent coach is self-awareness. By definition, self-awareness is recognizing how your emotions and behaviors are affecting other people in the moment. So, in the vignette above, Simon's failure to be aware of how he had answered the big question to his supervisor could put him at risk for making a mistake in judgment. A balance exists between intuition and reason, bringing recognition of strengths as well as areas of deficiency. Self-awareness is being able to accept feedback, knowing your system of values and knowing what you can achieve. Being confident in your own abilities, in what you can do or what you have done, is yet another trait of self-awareness.

Why is our awareness of self so critical? A conscious recognition of self is what, in part, defines our humanity. Think back to the introduction of the book with Tom and Susan. How would you rate Tom's self-awareness the moment Susan stepped into his office? Was he conscious enough of the tension he was feeling to have his full thinking mind available to make the best decision possible for Susan and for the firm?

We are the people who have the most influence over ourselves. Occasionally, we try to put this off onto other people by assuming the role of the "victim," but certainly we have the most control over ourselves and over our lives. This understanding of ourselves is the first step in our being able to make sense of our world. Self-awareness is what allows us to connect our values and beliefs to our behaviors. As a result, this awareness is what drives us, motivates us, and empowers us to be who we are as human beings.

As humans, we struggle with this concept of just being. We always have to be doing something, creating some value or enhancing our lives in some consumer-oriented way. Why is it that we cannot just sit and enjoy? What would it be like for you to just sink into a comfortable chair and slowly sip a cup of coffee on a warm day without the feeling of guilt or the need to be doing something? What would it take for you to just sit quietly and feel loved by someone? If you are a spiritual person, what would it require to just be still in a room for one hour and let God love you? If you are not spiritually inclined, what would it feel like to you to completely relax? Would you find this difficult? What if, instead of an hour, you just spent ten minutes doing such an exercise? Try it and see how you do just *being*. How is it that we put such great value on doing? The doing does not have to be anything important or critical; in fact, most of the time it is not.

One of my favorite cartoons is Dilbert. Have you ever been asked, like Dilbert has, to "attend a meeting that has no real purpose?" You've actually gone to such meetings and sat there for an hour or more, haven't you? We tend to justify our behavior: "I attended the meeting even thought I thought it was a waste of time" or "At the very least I'm doing something," we tell ourselves. "The boss wanted me to show up...so I did!" If we can spend an entire hour in a meeting that has no purpose, we need to be able to find ten minutes to just be human and become more aware of ourselves. We put such pressure on ourselves to perform, and in doing so, we often miss the joy that was intended for the journey.

Here is another self-awareness exercise for you to try. During a visit with an important client or customer (either internal or external), pause to consider what it would be like to be *him or her* for just a moment? To do this means you have so much confidence in yourself that you are comfortable momentarily leaving your own selfish thoughts and desires in order to try to understand the other person's struggles or concerns. To do this means you have a great self-awareness.

Have you ever had an intuition that you were right or wrong about something? Have you ever thought that, as you watch a situation evolve, you not only know what you would do but also why you would do it? You were experiencing emotional self-awareness. Authors Stein and Book, in *EQ Edge*, describe self-awareness as the "centerpiece" of emotional intelligence, because it is the attribute that allows you to understand and interact with the other attributes of emotional intelligence.

When the skill of emotional self-awareness is well developed, we are better able to interact with our environment. We have more confidence and self-assurance about who we are and our reason for being. Lane states that "One's ability to empathize cannot exceed one's ability to monitor one's own emotional state." This means that, as the centerpiece for emotional intelligence, we cannot give what we do not have. This competency is "rate limiting." In emotional intelligence terms, rate limiting is be defined as the element that will halt your growth because you have run out of it. To illustrate this concept of rate limiting, imagine shopping at the grocery store with $50 with intent to buy every item you see that costs one dollar. You would be able to buy 50 items before you run out of money because you are rate limited by the $50 you have in your pocket. Once the money is used up you cannot buy any more items. This is how emotional self-awareness works. You will not be able to show emotional intelligence beyond what you are capable of being aware of in the moment.

The Value of Self-Awareness in Coaching
In order to be able to coach others, there is typically work that first needs to be done on ourselves. If we are to be of value to those around us (work or family), we must be aware of our own emotional state. This is the efficiency that will allow us to help someone else complete their journey, assuming we are comfortable with and knowledgeable about our own selves. An executive once related a story to me about employing the services of a professional coach. The executive was feeling rather stuck in the goal-setting process that he and his team were developing and so wanted some outside perspective on the situation. At an initial meeting, this executive explained the problem for the coach. Instead of trying to help the executive understand where the road block had occurred, the coach sympathized with the executive about what a tough spot the executive was in! The coach seemed more concerned with how they were feeling about the situation than the predicament in which the executive and his team found themselves.

Predictably, the executive terminated the coaching relationship after two sessions. He left the relationship feeling very much like the coach never understood the situation with which he was faced. Had the coach been emotionally self-aware, he would have known that the primary goal was to help his client gain emotional awareness that would lead to a better understanding of the difficult situation at hand.

The value of self-awareness in coaching is difficult to overstate. As you become more aware of your body in relation to the other person, you will become more comfortable with yourself. You should also begin to work on how your thought processes are reacting. What are the things in your world causing you to have an emotional reaction? Can you identify them? If you can identify them, you will be able to work on managing them so as to become a more effective coach. As you increase your comfort and confidence, you will be more effective in developing the other efficiencies of emotional intelligence.

Self-Awareness Exercises:
1. Think about when you are in a conversation with your boss or spouse. What non-verbal communication directed at you should you be aware of? Are you able to pick up the energy that the other person is exhibiting? Have you ever been surprised by feedback? Journal your responses to the questions above.

2. Think critically: Perhaps you got fired, have been divorced, or failed to get a job that you really thought you were going to get. Were there warning signs you did not see? (*As you look back at your situation, you can see it now. But at the time you could not see it. Project that to your current situation. What are you not seeing now that you could or should be seeing? Are there things that are blinding you or that you are avoiding? What are you pretending not to see?*) Journal your responses.

3. Now look at the future. What disagreement or crisis is going to happen a day, week or month down the road that you can be most ready to respond to, that you can already see?

4. While sitting across from someone you trust, become aware of your emotions. As you are in conversation with and are still looking at them, hold your gaze on their face but use your peripheral vision. See if you can notice other things in the room, such as a painting, or a clock, or the color of the wall. Can you tell what time it is without breaking eye contact with the other person? Are you aware of the type of emotional response this creates in you? Here are some other physical characteristics to which you should pay attention:

   -What is your body position?

   -Are you smiling?

   -Where are your eyes moving?

   -Do you feel flushed in your face?

-Is your heart beating faster or slower?

-Is your skin sweating?

-Is your breathing shallow or deep?

SEVEN

Secret #2:
Authenticity

Rick, *a veteran restaurant manager, knew he could not rest on the by-gone ideas about serving customers that had served him so well over the years. Rick believed his new boss when she said that trust was something that took a lifetime to earn, yet could be lost in an instant. Rick translated this thought into everything he did with customers. He continually preached "serve the customer" to his team.*

Rick believed he had a firm understanding of a key principle of the restaurant business: success depended greatly upon the loyalty of the customer. As the manager, he was dependent upon that loyal customer base returning again and again. Rick had learned that patrons came back not just for the food. After all, they could get beef, chicken, or fish just about anywhere. What the customer couldn't get just anywhere else was the experience of a hospitable wait staff that promptly seated them and then waited on them like kings and queens. The difference was the staff that Rick had hired and trained and motivated over the years.

The staff was motivated largely as a result of how Rick managed. He would thank them in public, but if they needed a correction he would pull them aside in a private area. Rick told himself that this was what he loved most about this very public business. He deeply enjoyed and valued the staff that worked so hard. He especially appreciated seeing the extra effort and commitment he received from them in return. This extra effort and commitment from the staff was always noticed and rewarded by his supervisors over the years.

Rick was ruminating on all of this during his last day in his job. He also understood that his own motivation was greatly influenced by his own supervisor. Unfortunately, with a new boss, things had come unraveled. While Rick believed his new supervisor when she talked about the dynamics of trust, he just didn't see any of it from her.

Rick had observed too many inconsistencies. He realized that no one is perfect, but the different standard under which he was expected to work was too difficult to overcome. The new boss would come in late while talking with everyone on the staff about giving an honest day's work for an honest day's pay. She constantly preached about work effort, yet most of the time she herself was nowhere to be found. Working from home is what she called it. "How in the world can you run a people business from home?" Rick asked himself.

Then there were the budget cuts. First to go were the waitresses Rick had hired to serve drinks while people waited. "No other restaurant was doing this any longer," she would say in justifying her actions. Next came cutting the hostess staffing from two down to one per shift. Rick had staffed this way to ensure that every customer would be greeted by a smiling face and a kind word. "Lack of productivity" and "duplication of efforts" were the comments from the new boss.

At first, Rick bought into the "higher profitability, new way of doing things." But as he reflected on nearly twenty years of service, he found himself in a real dilemma. His success was a clear threat to this new executive, such that if she had not made changes, then she likely would have been labeled as "nonprogressive." Rick was convinced if he made the changes his new boss advocated, the business was doomed.

Rick felt that all he had left were his values and his integrity. Even if the new boss left soon, once Rick compromised on his principles, he knew he couldn't continue to work there. And so, he had resigned. Several of the staffers had already told him that they very much wanted to work for him again when he landed at a new restaurant. Rick felt conflicted about this but resigned himself to the belief that all would be fine in the end.

How is it in our organizations that we so often lose the best and the brightest? Certainly, we can manage our organizations with less than the best. But can we really thrive?

Authenticity in Coaching

The second secret of an emotionally intelligent coach is authenticity. In conducting this research to discover the attributes that great coaches possess, *authenticity* was paramount to those being coached. Exhibiting true authenticity first requires that we have a grasp of our own personal value system, that we understand those things for which we stand. When we know what is genuinely important to us and what is absolutely significant in our lives, the decisions that we must make are anchored in those values.

We are all faced with situations in life in which our values are challenged. With the clients I have the privilege to coach, this often creates the greatest source of personal tension for them. For example, it's easy to *say* that honesty is one of the things that we most value in life. Most of us would admit that we are occasionally tempted, and that sometimes we even stray from being honest. If honesty is really a value of ours, we probably wouldn't walk into a retail store and stuff our pockets full of candy, would we? Yet, how many of us have, at one time or another, downloaded a song off of the Internet and not paid for it? We recently had to have this discussion within our own family. My son had discovered a copy of a movie on the Internet that had not yet been released. Our conversation centered around the idea that just because the Internet is full of "free" information, that does not mean that all information or, in this case, entertainment, is free. Thinking that no one will ever succumb to this kind of temptation is simply ridiculous. Likely, you have known several people with the highest level of integrity who have found themselves in hot water as a result of suppressing information or failing to tell the entire truth.

Authentic trust must be earned in a coaching relationship. This is a nonnegotiable. One of the ways this is borne out in my own coaching is that I place high value on honoring my commitments. Another way this plays out for me is that I am a stickler in being on time for scheduled appointments. I simply do not like being late or canceling at the last minute. To do so, in my book, demonstrates disrespect to my clients when I am late to an appointment. Sure, I know things happen and people get stuck in traffic; sometimes there are flight delays. In cases like these, it's important to me to call to explain that I am late. However, just because I value commitment doesn't mean that everyone else values it the way I do.

Building trust with those we coach is a prerequisite to accomplishing anything of substance. Until your coachees are absolutely convinced that you have their best interests at heart and that you genuinely care about them, they are not likely to buy in to many things that you may wish to share with them. And they will be even more reluctant to accept criticism, even that of a constructive nature.

Ethics in Coaching
Authentic trust must be preserved in a coaching relationship. What does that look like? Well, the International Coach Federation (www.coachfederation.org) lists some 28 key points in four major categories, all of which speak directly to the issue of ethical conduct in the coaching environment. ICF identifies areas like conduct with clients and conduct "at large" as having separate and distinct ethical guidelines. Many of these seem, on the surface, to be obvious. Yet, the need for being intentional about spelling out such guidelines is also obvious. Guiding principles include things like personal conduct, honesty, a respect for various approaches to coaching, and handling information with

confidentiality in mind. Other important topics speak to things like setting boundaries; refusing to become sexually involved with a client; avoid intentionally misleading others; and, referring a client to a different coach when such an action would be in the client's best interest.

Familiarize yourself with the issues that face coaches. There are many of them. The trust that you hold with another individual is not unlike a form of power or influence over them. You simply cannot abuse that relationship for any reason.

Consistency

Consistency is crucial to creating authentic trust when coaching. The mortal enemy of consistency in a trusting relationship is hypocrisy. What coaches fear most is giving direction to a coachee but then feeling like they were talking directly to themselves. In a *Time* magazine article dated May 14, 2007, entitled, "Why Scandals Stick," the author made an extremely insightful point: "Hypocrisy isn't a crime. It's more like a sad song sung in the round: you forgot to practice what you preach."

Many of us may well identify with the frustration surrounding the inconsistency that former World Bank president Paul Wolfowitz exhibited in his executive role there. As the former U.S. Deputy Secretary of Defense and the principal architect of the 2003 invasion of Iraq, Wolfowitz created many enemies. Ultimately, his critics chased him out of the Pentagon. Much to the surprise of the Washington pundits, in 2005 Wolfowitz wound up as president of the World Bank on a platform of declaring war on poverty and corruption. He proceeded to deliver on this promise by increasing the wealth of his girlfriend, charitably giving her a $60,000 raise. Critics again cried foul, asking how Wolfowitz could possibly fight corruption abroad when he apparently had failed to fight it within himself.

Certainly, such behavior is not tolerable. Time will tell if Wolfowitz is, in fact, guilty as publicly charged. If so, he should endure the consequences. However, I can truly empathize with Wolfowitz. I can understand the conflict that comes with being a leader. I can appreciate declaring a stance on terrible things like world poverty and corruption but then not examining my own life closely enough to see where my own values are inconsistent with my behaviors. It pretty much happens to most, if not all of us, at one point or another, doesn't it?

An example of this inner conflict in my own coaching career has surfaced with several clients I coach. One of the fairly consistent struggles in the lives of the executives with whom I work is their work-life balance. These days, people commonly overcommit, underdeliver and then feel a lot of internal conflict. My clients feel like they can't say "no" to anyone, else their careers are on the line. Hour after hour, I have spent listening to such stories in trying to help people work through this inner conflict. At the end of the coaching session, I typically assign clients who struggle with this issue some exercises upon which they can work. You will find similar exercises at the end of this chapter.

Often, I leave these coaching situations feeling like I have given considerable value to the clients I am coaching, only to notice the same conflict in myself. How do I get everything done? How do I meet my publisher's deadlines, coach my clients, speak to thousands of people a year, and deliver coaching training to thousands more and yet not resolve this conflict in my own professional life?

Confidentiality
Private conversations deserve private locations. Confidentiality in coaching is vital to creating authentic trust with your clients. It's a fairly simple concept: keep the details of the coaching session to yourself. Whether you are a professional coach or one who works with colleagues in the corporate sector, client issues may be similar or they may be different. Regardless, they must be kept confidential. There are few ways to lose your credibility faster than to betray your clients' confidences.

Commitment

Vital to the process of building an authentically trusting organization is commitment to your coachees and their well being. Bill George, author of *True North: Discover Your Authentic Leadership,* writes: "During the past 50 years, leadership scholars have conducted more than one thousand studies in an attempt to determine definitive styles, characteristics, or personality traits of great leaders." (George, et al. 129)

The point is that you cannot be authentic while trying to be like someone else. While, no doubt, you can learn from other leaders' experiences, genuine authenticity comes from practicing the values and principles these leaders have acquired through life's experiences.

Rob Goffee and Gareth Jones, in their book *Managing Authenticity,* agree with George. They take the principle idea one step further, however, by insisting that the establishment of authenticity is a two-part challenge. The first hurdle entails ensuring that the words you speak match your actions. Goffee and Jones attribute this quality to being consistent over time in word and in deed. A leader knows what he believes and carries out this belief in what he says and how he acts each and every day.

The second barrier to overcome is that of finding common ground with those in your "follower-ship." Goffee and Jones define this as treating people and people groups differently. At times, this can be difficult to integrate with the attribute of authenticity, especially when trying to find ways to identify with others.

We've established that authenticity is about knowing ourselves well enough to be *real.* We must make decisions consistent with our value system. As such, we know our values system and are comfortable with the relationship our values have in decision making.

Our values construct can have many influences: spiritual, family, mental, physical, professional growth, workplace, community, etc. A very useful tool on this topic is a values wheel, which you may read more about in the book, "Leading Change in Your World", by Mark Smith and Larry Lindsay.

The Value of Authenticity in Coaching

Authenticity is about being open and honest with yourself when presenting to others. Don't get focused on being who your coachees want you to be, but rather who you truly are. If there is a difference between how you feel and what you express, you may need a little work in the area of authenticity.

What do you most avoid talking about with your boss, your spouse or your kids? What do you want to say, but you're simply not saying? What dreams or desires do you have in your heart but you avoid? In your last conversation, do you wish you had said something, but didn't? Why not? Could it have been a fear of rejection? Failure? Might you be concerned about what others think or a loss of control?

Authenticity Exercises:
1. Take five minutes to write down the things in life you value most. Be specific and descriptive. Often, it is helpful to string two or three such things together. Brainstorm about these. Then review your list, identifying and circling the three that occur most often. Now link these three together in a string that becomes your prioritized list. Again, review. Consider if there are any other values that you would add to these three. For the purposes of this exercise, try to limit the count to five or six (recognizing, of course, that you value more than this list in your life). Finally, write a one-sentence description for each of the values you've listed describing how you like this value to be shown in your life.

Example of a Value String: Honesty/Integrity/Commitment
Example of Value Sentence: I honor commitments by returning
phone calls in 24 hours.

Now it is time to solicit feedback from others. Share what you've written with people you know to ask them if they feel the sentences accurately describe you. *Do you notice any gaps from the feedback you are given by others?*

2. After you have created and received feedback on your value sentences, spend some time examining your life. Do you notice any current conflicts you are having with your values? If so, which ones? In a journal, write to yourself. Create an action plan to forgive yourself for not living up to your values. *(Don't give up if this seems a little difficult at first. It will be worth it!)* How does writing a forgiveness plan to yourself make you feel? What action steps have you decided to take after forgiving yourself for not living up to your values? Finally, are there any barriers to trust that impact your ability to coach?

EIGHT

Secret #3: Optimism

Keri couldn't believe it! She was scheduled for the third of twelve executive coaching sessions with Jack, the fiery Chief of Police. But Jack was nowhere to be found. No one in the office had any idea where Jack was, nor did he respond to any phone messages. Jack had been about half an hour late for their first meeting, a fact that Keri attributed to the role of a busy executive. But when Jack failed to show up on two separate occasions for their scheduled meetings, Keri thought there may be some problem.

The Springfield Police Department had contracted with Keri to coach Jack for two reasons. First, she was a local expert in the area of emotional intelligence, an area that Jack became interested in after a Chamber of Commerce meeting. Jack thought he could use some help with keeping his "full thinking mind," as the speaker had explained it, during times of tension and complexity. Jack was also interested in obtaining Keri's coaching skills due to the fact that she was unfamiliar with police work. Jack knew enough about police work for at least two people, after some thirty years of dedicated service. He was really interested in learning something new, a fresh perspective on leadership.

As Keri sat in Jack's office waiting on her coachee to eventually *appear at the door, she started to have an internal conversation. Keri knew this was a conversation that people have with themselves when things don't go as expected. Despite the fact that Keri knew she needed to control her thinking during times like this, those "negative" thoughts just kept flooding her head. Her thought patterns were not terribly unlike some of the people she had coached. She kept thinking: "Why is Jack continually missing appointments with me? It seems to always end up this way with new clients; they miss the first appointment, and it's the most important one! My entire coaching career will probably end up this way. How frustrating!"*

It was amazing to Keri how fast this kind of thinking overtook her. She knew better than to think this way. The truth was: Jack was not continually missing appointments. This was only the second time and he is the Chief of Police for a large metropolitan area. This did not happen every time she had a new client. As she recounted, this was merely the third out of almost fifteen clients with which this was an issue. She should follow her dream! She had many frustrations with this client, but at the end of the day she could reflect on the fact that she loved her job!

As Keri left Jack's office, she placed a note on his chair and left another voice message indicating that she was sorry they had missed their time. She suggested that Jack call her to reschedule. She knew that she would have to be the one, however, to initiate the call.

The third secret of an emotionally intelligent coach is optimism. When you think about the word *optimism*, what kinds of thoughts generally come to mind? In the space provided below, write down what comes into your mind when you hear the word optimism:

_____

_____

_____

If you are like most people we interviewed in conducting the research for this chapter, you wrote something about a feeling that everything is going to turn out well. Optimism is a generalized disposition to expect the best out of every situation. Optimists view life by looking upon the world as a *positive* place. Optimists generally believe that people are inherently good. Such individuals believe that, given sufficient time, things will work out in the end. A common example used to illustrate optimism is this question: Is a drinking glass that contains liquid equal to 50 percent of its capacity *half full* or *half empty?*

By definition, this isn't a bad place to start. In some respects, optimism does have something to do with positive feelings. When it came to working with coaches, however, our research uncovered something quite interesting. The definition of optimism is broader than just a general feeling that "everything will eventually work out." Coaches recognize instead that it is unrealistic to assume that *everything* will *always* work out. As we know in life, things do *not* always work out the way we want them to work out.

In fact, many of the coaches we interviewed termed this unrealistic view of optimism as "pollyanna-ism." Do you recall the story of Pollyanna? Pollyanna Whittier is a young girl who, after her father's death, must move in with her wealthy Aunt Polly to live. Pollyanna's philosophy of life centers around what she calls "The Glad Game." She always tries to find something about which to be glad in every situation and always tries to do without delay whatever she thinks is right. With this philosophy, and her own sunny personality, she brings much gladness to her aunt's dispirited New England town, transforming it into a pleasant, healthy place to live. Eventually, however, even Pollyanna's robust optimism is put to the test when she loses the use of her legs in an accident.

In general, this is the problem most people have with eternally optimistic coaches. Can a person possess a generally good feeling that everything is going to turn out alright when the news is bad? Optimism is fairly easy when things are going well, but when adversity strikes, what happens then? What happens then? An optimistic coach would suggest that rarely is it as bad as it seems. People often try to convince themselves it is.

New Frame for Optimism

As coaches, rather than being stuck in the frame work of "glass half full" or "Pollyanna," we need a different paradigm for optimism. As coaches (and human beings), we are constantly talking to ourselves. It is this self-talk we now explore, as we apply the efficiency of optimism to coaching. How many of us have ever taken the time to think about our *thought* lives? We spend a considerable amount of time with ourselves, having conversations with ourselves inside our own heads. We talk to ourselves much more than we converse with any other person on the planet. What do those conversations with yourself sound like when you are coaching? When things are going well as a coach, how do you talk to yourself? When your coaching efforts are *not* going as you would like, what kinds of things do you tell yourself? This internal conversation we have with ourselves is our thought life. The internal thought life can have a tremendous impact on coaches and the people they serve. This thought life has the potential to impact many actions that are taken, or aren't taken, during the course of a day. This thought life is termed *"explanatory style"* by author Martin Seligman in what is sure to become a psychological classic entitled, *Learned Optimism: How to Change Your Mind and Your Life.* Our coaching thought life (or how we explain things to ourselves) may take the form of optimism or pessimism. To understand the distinction between optimistic self-talk and pessimistic self-talk, we must examine *how* we talk to ourselves about three different dimensions of our lives: our self, time and scope. (Important: bear in mind that we are talking about *how* we talk to ourselves, not outcomes. Do not fall into the trap of measuring outcomes or results as we discuss this topic. In moving through this chapter, remember that the discussion is framed around the conversations you have with yourself.)

Self

As an optimistic coach talks to himself, he will understand when to take responsibility for what is in his control and distinguish this from what is outside his control. Taking responsibility is the key point here. Giving an account of your actions or taking responsibility for the discharge of a duty or trust is critically important. Are you really responsible for the action or event? As you talk to yourself, if the event is in your control and you take responsibility for it, regardless of consequences or outcome, this is characterized as optimistic self-talk. Likewise, if an event is negative or out of your control, yet you do not accept responsibility for the outcome or thought, this is also viewed as an optimistic response. Pessimistic self-talk, on the other hand, is framed as not accepting responsibility for good events in our control. Pessimistic self talk is also described as when bad events occur that are out of our control and yet we still take responsibility.

Time

An optimistic coach will understand when they talk to themselves just how permanent is the event in time. How we view our conversation within the realm of time is critical to obtaining optimistic self-talk. If you tend toward optimistic self-talk, you are likely to view positive events in time as more permanent and negative events in time as more temporary. If your style of self-talk is more pessimistic, you tend to view positive events in time as temporary and negative events in time as more permanent.

Scope

An optimistic coach will understand when they talk to themselves just how pervasive is the event. How we view our conversation within the realm of extent is vital as we learn to talk optimistically to ourselves. If you lean toward optimistic self-talk, you tend to view positive events as happening frequently and having a lasting effect. Similarly, optimistic self-talk will view negative events as temporary setbacks. By contrast, pessimistic self-talk tends to view positive events as temporary or rarely occurring in life and negative or bad events as happening more frequently and having a more permanent length.

Self-Talk Framing Chart

Positive or good event	Optimistic self-talk	Pessimistic self-talk
Self	Take responsibility	Responsibility lies outside of me
Time	Sense of permanence	Temporary
Scope	Pervasive to similar events	Restricted to event
Negative or bad event	**Optimistic self-talk**	**Pessimistic self-talk**
Self	Able to distinguish what responsible for and what is outside area of responsibility	Takes responsibility even if source of accountability lies elsewhere
Time	Temporary setback	Sense of permanence
Scope	Restricted to event	Pervasive to other events

Now, to gain insight into this dynamic of self-talk, let us use the story at the beginning of the chapter with a different scenario. For example, let's assume that Jack showed up to Keri's appointment on time. From Keri's perspective, this would have been a positive event. Reflecting back on the Self- Talk Framing Chart, fill in the chart below as to what you think Keri's self-talk would have been if she had an optimistic self-talk style or a pessimistic self-talk style. I have included an example immediately following this exercise in order to provide you with a reference point for your answers.

Jack is on time for meeting with Keri; A positive or good event	Optimistic self-talk	Pessimistic self-talk
Self		
Time		
Scope		

Jack is on time for meeting with Keri; A positive or good event	Optimistic self-talk	Pessimistic self-talk
Self	I am a good coach	My coachees don't value my efforts
Time	Jack is on time	Jack is on time today
Scope	Coachees value my time	Jack values my time

Now that you have mastered self-talk for positive events, let us attempt the same exercise for the story at the beginning of this chapter as it happened, a perceived negative event. Assume that events happen as originally written in the narrative, meaning that Jack didn't show up for Keri's appointment on time. From Keri's perspective, this would be a negative event. Fill in the chart as to what you think Keri's optimistic self-talk and pessimistic self-talk would look like. I have included an example immediately following this exercise so you can check your answers.

Jack is late for meeting with Keri; a negative or bad event	Optimistic self-talk	Pessimistic self-talk
Self		
Time		
Scope		

Jack is late for meeting with Keri; a negative or bad event	Optimistic self-talk	Pessimistic self-talk
Self	Jack is a busy man	My clients all run late
Time	Jack is late today	My clients are always late
Scope	Jack is wasting my time	This is a waste of my time

How do you talk to or explain things to yourself? What kinds of things as a coach do you tell yourself about those you coach? What are the conversations *you have with you* about yourself? Here is an added bonus: What kinds of thoughts do you have about the person on this earth whom you love the most?

Here is another exercise to develop your coaching knowledge on the topic of optimism and your thought life. Reflect upon the following scenarios for a few moments, and then complete the following chart:

Coachee: *Think about the best thing that has happened to you within the past seven days with a person you coach.*

Self: *Think about the best thing that has happened to you personally within the past seven days.*

Person you love: *Think about the best interaction you have had with the one person you love the most within the past seven days.*

Record in the chart below, as best you can, the thoughts you had immediately following these positive events. To make this exercise meaningful, it is critically important that you are *honest* with yourself and that you record what it is you were actually thinking. Resist the temptation to record what you did. The goal is to consider your thought life, not the actions you took.

After you have completed the positive event on the left side of the chart, we are going to ask the same three questions so you can complete the negative thought life column on the right side of the chart.

Coachee: *Think about the worst thing that has happened to you with a person you coach within the past seven days.*

Self: *Think about the worst thing that has happened to you personally within the past seven days.*

Person you love: *Think about the worst interaction you have had with the one person you love the most within the past seven days.*

	Thought life after a positive event	Thought life after a negative event
Coachee		
Self		
Person you love		

Do you notice any difference between the two columns? Are there any patterns you notice in your thought life? How do you view positive and negative things that happen to you? How do you view your accountability as a coach? What impact does time or permanence have on your thought life? Did you notice anything about the scope or pervasiveness you placed on events?

As you consider this thought life, it is very useful to consider *how* you frame these events. Write in the space below any thoughts you have had about *how* you talk to yourself when you view events as positive or negative. I have provided space for you to think about someone you are currently coaching, yourself, and someone you love.

Current coachee	Thought life after a positive event	Thought life after a negative event
Self		
Time		
Scope		

Self	Thought life after a positive event	Thought life after a negative event
Self		
Time		
Scope		

Someone you love	Thought life after a positive event	Thought life after a negative event
Self		
Time		
Scope		

Take a few minutes to peruse the three charts you have created and then write down any common themes you find in your thought life between a current coachee, yourself and the person you love, with respect to *A positive event* or *A negative event*.

Common themes	Thought life after a positive event	Thought life after a negative event
Self		
Time		
Scope		

Take a moment to journal your thoughts on what you have learned about framing positive or negative events in your own thought life:

_____

_____

_____

Dread Zone

One final concept is worth considering as we explore how we talk to ourselves. When it comes to pessimistic self-talk, several of my executive clients have described a negative spiral that spins downwardly and out of control. I call this process *rabbit thoughts* because we start with one or two negative thoughts and then we link them. Before we know it, they have multiplied out of control. This place of multiplied, negative self-talk is what I call the *dread zone*. Most of what we are telling ourselves is not based in truth or reality. A client of mine recounted the following story, as an example:

I learned that I needed to take an unexpected business trip. My wife and I routinely put together our work and social calendars at least a month in advance, so when this trip came up, I began to experience some dread. My thoughts, initially, revolved around how important this trip was to my business. Then I started thinking about something my wife once said to me about how important my business is to me. Next, I found myself mentally defending my business trip, yet how my wife would be disappointed with my decision to take it in light of the fact that our monthly calendar was already set. The next thought I had was that of walking in the door and ignoring my wife so that I could avoid the conflict of the trip. I envisioned our not speaking with each other all night. I was about ready to explode at my wife's insensitivity to my needs for a successful business.

Suddenly, I realized that I was in the "dread zone." None of these thoughts upon which I had been dwelling was true. I hadn't even talked to my wife about this trip. Immediately, I paused and used the Five R's of Optimistic Response. Then I walked in the door, kissed my wife, and told her about the trip. She responded by telling me how proud of me that she was, and expressed appreciation for how far I had come in my career. Of course, she was disappointed that a dinner with friends would need to be moved. But she understood.

The *dread zone* can be a terrible place to be for coaches. When the *rabbit thoughts* start to multiply, the thoughts can seem to spin hopelessly out of control. As you examine the story above, where did the *rabbit thoughts* start? And exactly why did the *rabbit thoughts* start? Which emotional need was not met in this instance that caused the executive to defend his actions?

Outcomes rarely play out as we fear they may when we are in this place. Just imagine if the client above had walked in and projected this *dread zone* thinking onto his family situation. What a disastrous outcome could have occurred! If you find your self-talk taking you to the *dread zone* more often than you would like, you may find the following model useful as you endeavor to climb your way out!

Five R's of Optimism Development

As I have worked with coachees over the course of the last several years, a useful model for optimism has evolved that I have implemented in my own coaching practice. I believe you will find it useful, as well, in developing your own optimism. This process does require purposeful and intentional practice. Needless to say, this is not something that you can read once in a book and then expect it to become second nature. I strongly encourage you to identify those areas of your life where you find yourself in the *dread zone*. These seats of pessimistic self-talk represent opportunities for immediate and profound changes in ourselves as coaches.

Step 1 - Report Facts: Describe the facts of the situation to yourself. What *actually* happened? Be careful to report only what is real to your situation. Resist the temptation to predict the future of what could happen as an outcome. You only want *the facts* in this step.

Step 2 - Recount Emotion: Write down the emotions you felt. We will use them in the next step. The more you are able to recognize *all* of the emotions involved, the better you will be able to sort through those that deserve your efforts in changing your view of the situation.

Step 3 - Result of Emotion: This step attaches a consequence to the emotional impact you are feeling when you are in the *dread zone*. Use language like, "(Event), I felt_____. This caused me to (*dread zone*)_____." This process serves to attach a cognitive outcome to your feelings. Here's an example: "Because Jack was late for our appointment (Event), I felt disrespected. This caused me to (enter the *dread zone*) think that none of my clients respect my time."

Step 4 - Ruckus: In this step, you need to create controversy within my your self-talk. The solution is to quite literally argue that your negative self-talk is not serving you at this time. The *dread zone* is no place for you to live and so you need to move out *right now*.

Many executive coaching clients have a good deal of fun with this step. After completing the sentence in step 3 (the Result of Emotion), the error of thought that our emotion has caused often becomes apparent. It's at this point that we often realize the silliness of our *dread zone* position. The solution is as simple as creating a little chaos for ourselves at the end of this negative self-talk. We break the pattern by asking ourselves why our thought on this event has any relevance to other life situations.

This ruckus might be expressed like this: "(Event), I felt_____. This caused me to (*dread zone*) _____ (Argument)_____." For example, "Because Jack was late for our appointment (Event), I felt disrespected. This caused me to (enter the *dread zone*) think that none of my clients respect my time (initiate Argument). Why should Jack being late have anything to do with any of my other clients?" We can also begin to feel how good it is to win this argument with ourselves and start our move out of the *dread zone*.

Step 5 - Refocus: It is now time to begin the journey out of the *dread zone*. You have finished the self-argument and now can see the error of your logic. It is time to rewrite the sentence in step 3 to a more optimistic self-talk. For example, "(Event) Because Jack was late for our appointment, I felt disrespected. This caused me to (enter the *dread zone*) think that none of my clients respect my time (Argument). Why should Jack being late have anything to do with any of my other clients?" (Refocus) Jack is late because Jack has many priorities. I should ask him how he is prioritizing this coaching that he hired me to do.

Now, you try it. Identify a situation that lands you in the *dread zone*, and then practice using the *Five R's of Optimism Development*.

	Dread Zone Situation
Report facts	
Recount emotion	
Result of emotion	
Ruckus	
Refocus	

The value of your optimistic self-talk is vital to those you coach. The belief you possess within yourself as a professional is transferable and impactful. Pulling yourself out of the *dread zone* has great potential to completely change your coaching outlook.

The Value of Optimism in Coaching

From our research, we learned that an optimistic coach is of more value to a coachee than a pessimistic coach. The people we interviewed replied that the value of having a coach who recognizes adversity and yet transfers feelings of strong hope is immeasurable. A coach who believes in himself or herself is able to transmit this dominant emotion to the person being coached.

Optimism for coaches then comes down to resiliency. It is not *if* we are going to deal with a setback in our coaching, but rather *when* we will experience a setback in our coaching. How we respond to these setbacks depends not upon the event at hand, but how we talk to ourselves during these events. Therefore, when a setback does occur, how can you as a coach frame the issue so as to have more optimistic self-talk? What can you do to develop your optimistic self-talk so that this positive transference of belief can occur for those who are in your leadership realm?

Optimism Exercises:

1. Continue to examine situations where you talk to yourself. Complete the exercises in the chapter to examine your level of optimism. Study the results to observe any thought patterns you commonly have as you talk to yourself.

2. Read *Learned Optimism: How To Change Your Mind and Your Life,* by Martin Seligman. You will find many excellent "life examples" in this work, along with some diagnostic self-tests that will enable you to learn more about your prominent thinking style.

3. Identify *dread zone* areas in your life. Watch your thought patterns over the next week. Can you identify any places where you find yourself falling into the *dread zone*? Use the Five R's of Optimism Development to work on escaping the *dread zone*.

NINE

Secret #4:
Impulse Control

"**D**id you see that email from Peter?" Cindy said to her boss, Ted. Only three lines in length, the words could have been made from tungsten and sharpened with steel the way they cut into Cindy:

To: Kevin <kevin.jones@acmecorp.com>
From: Peter<peter.smith@acmecorp.com>
Cc: Cindy <cindy.glover@acmecorp.com>, Ted <ted.sales@acmecorp.com>

Re: Pass code for Kevin's security access

Kevin,

Cindy keeps telling me your security access expires next month. I know you told me it is good for another year but I was just in a meeting and Cindy said it was due to expire. Can you make a copy of your security badge and give it to me so Cindy will get off my back?

Thanks,
Peter

It was that last sentence that really got under Cindy's skin. One of Cindy's responsibilities at her firm was to make sure all employees had access to the building via the new security system. The only reason she had brought up the issue of Kevin's security access with Peter was to make certain Kevin could get in the door in the morning. Furthermore, Cindy thought, she was NOT "on his back". She was merely letting Peter know so that everyone on the team had access to the building.

Ted, Cindy's boss, said, "Cindy, let me give you some coaching. You two need to work this out. Set up a meeting with Peter and work things out."

"Coaching?" Cindy thought. "That was not coaching…that was a directive." Cindy was so angry that she couldn't think straight. She knew from all of the management seminars she had attended that she needed to create some options and then try to understand the consequences of each decision prior to implementation. She felt like she still needed to talk to someone. Maybe her best friend, Denise, could calm her down. Perhaps Denise could help her with some real coaching that would put her on the right road.

The fourth secret of an emotionally intelligent coach is impulse control. Calling Denise is a good idea for Cindy because at this stage of the situation, she really needs a coach, someone to listen to her and help her generate options from her thinking mind. Cindy needs someone who can help her sift through all of the emotions that are running through her mind and body. Which emotions would you be feeling right now if you were Cindy? Take a moment to write them down in the space below. I urge you not to skip over this, but to engage emotionally in this story. Doing so will help you better relate to this efficiency of impulse control:

_____

_____

_____

Coaching is not just about giving feedback, although feedback certainly can be one gift that a coach can provide.

Coaching is not about telling the other person what to do; it is about enabling him or her to discover how to envision and take a course of action on their own. Coaching is not teaching, although coaching can have an element of self-discovered learning as one component.

Do you find yourself falling into the trap of giving feedback without assisting the other person in exploring solutions? Do you catch yourself at times leaving the room thinking you were the smartest person in that meeting? Have you ever told someone exactly what to do with crystal clear accuracy, only to have him or her *not* do it right…again?

While feedback, advice, or even teaching can be valuable tools, they are not coaching. When offering advice or teaching someone, often the real object of the lesson becomes the advisor or the teacher. The focus of the relationship becomes: *do you understand what I am telling you?* The focus of coaching should be: *do you understand what you are hearing (seeing/feeling) and are you able to implement a behavior change as a result?*

I am not suggesting that there aren't valuable times for a coach to give advice. I'm certainly not saying that there are not teachable moments in life. Surely there are appropriate moments for these! They just should not be confused with coaching. The legendary Alabama Head Football Coach Paul Bear Bryant used as his measure of coaching success: "If anything goes bad, I did it. If anything goes good, we did it. If anything works out great, they did it."

What might it take for you to develop this type of philosophy as a coach? What are the challenges that lie ahead for you? Is it more important to you that others hear what you have to say or that they have an understanding of what you mean? Is it more important when leaving a meeting that you know you have been heard, or is it more important that others can implement your vision? It is NOT about you as the coach. Rather, it is about those you are coaching. If your coachee wins, you win. So what must you do to put yourself in a position where you win through them rather than over the top of them?

For many of us, this is *impulse control.* Sure, impulse control can be characterized as not yelling at the guy in traffic who cuts you off for no apparent reason. The first emotional reaction that typically surfaces in times of tension or complexity is one of anger or hostility toward the other driver. After all, this is our protection mechanism. This is an impulse control that deals with an unmet social need and usually expresses itself as anger or rage.

Likely, there are times when your employees or your kids make you feel this way. Impulse control strategies can be useful during such times. As a coach, however, I would challenge you to think beyond your times of anger. Instead, focus on those situations when you are in a coachable moment with a child or with an employee.

Self-awareness is about recognizing an emotion; impulse control is about managing the emotion so you have all of your options available to you. *(When emotion is exhibited incorrectly, it is typically perceived as anger or some unmet social need. Or, it is "swallowed" and the truth is never shared.)* Critical to this process is an awareness of those things that trigger our emotions, followed by the behavior that is our most skilled response. Consider that it may be more appropriate to delay the gratification that comes with articulating our best responses at a particular moment.

Perhaps the best known example of delayed gratification and the impact of impulse control comes from Stanford University psychology researcher Walter Mischel. In a longitudinal study begun in the 1960s, Mischel offered unsuspecting, yet eager, four-year-olds a marshmallow but told them that if they would wait for the researcher to return after running an errand, they would be given *two* marshmallows. Those who could manage to wait the requisite fifteen or twenty minutes for the return of the adult would be recognized as demonstrating the ability to delay gratification and control impulse. One-third of the children grabbed the single marshmallow right away, while some waited a little longer before taking the tempting morsel. Only one-third of the children were able to wait the necessary minutes so as to achieve the 100% increase in "prize money:" two marshmallows, rewarded to them for demonstrating impulse control.

The researchers of this study followed up with these same children when they graduated from high school. The differences between the two groups of kids were dramatic. Those who had been able to show impulse control and delay gratification for the allotted time were more positive, self-motivating, persistent in the face of difficulties, and were able to delay gratification in pursuit of their goals. Overall, they had acquired the habits of successful people that resulted in more successful marriages, higher incomes, greater career satisfaction, better health, and more fulfilling lives than most of the population.

Predictably, those children who had not demonstrated impulse control (by failing to wait for the return of the researcher), turned out to be more troubled, stubborn, indecisive, mistrustful, and less self-confident. They simply had been unable to put off gratification. This group struggled with delaying gut reactions and immediate impulses to achieve long-range goals. As an example, when it was time for these kids to study for tests, they tended to be easily distracted into doing activities that brought instant gratification. This impulse followed them throughout their lives and resulted in a higher percentage of unsuccessful marriages, low job satisfaction ratings and lower income achievement. This even extended to their overall health, which did not measure up to those others who had learned early on to delay gratification, including increased feelings of and more frequent frustration than the first group.

Impulse control enables us to weather any storm that comes our way. Consider it to be the mechanism whereby we take a "big picture" perspective of things. Impulse control is *not* about suppression of emotion; it is about managing it. You can enhance the impulse control in yourself. The next time your impulse is triggered, the key is to think of others and what they are experiencing while you are reacting. To do so means to let go of self, to let go of your own needs long enough to focus on the needs of others.

The Value of Impulse Control in Coaching

The value of impulse control for us as coaches is the empowerment we acquire to weather any storm that comes our way. Consider impulse control to be the mechanism whereby we take a "big picture" perspective of things. Impulse control is *not* about suppression of emotion, it is about managing it. Therefore, when we are with our coachees and we feel our bodies starting to *trigger*, our self-awareness nudges us and suggests that we are having an emotional reaction. This is our opportunity to realize that we may not be in the best place, mentally, to coach. We need to step back from this initial, knee-jerk reaction and maintain our comprehensive view of things. As we are able to do this as coaches, we place ourselves in a far better position to actually help the person we are there to coach.

As coaches, we also bear a responsibility to our clients to help them control their impulses. We need to be sensitive to body language, tone of voice, eye and facial expression. When we sense that our coachees are triggered emotionally, we can assist them in gaining their full thinking mind by asking thoughtful, caring, inquisitive questions. Questioning is a technique that will actually calm the amygdala and give our coachees more presence in the moment. This may, in fact, mean that we help them recognize the value of delaying gratification, even if this gratification is a knee-jerk response.

You will discover that it is possible to enhance impulse control in yourself and your coachees first by paying attention to those situations where the emotional impact is felt physically (in the body). The next time your impulse is triggered, the key response should be to think of others and what they are experiencing before you react. To do so means to let go of self, to let go of your own needs long enough to focus on the needs of others. Impulse control is the step between self-awareness and empathy. If you can control the impulsiveness you feel, then you can reach out to serve and benefit those

whom you coach and lead.
Impulse Control Exercises:
1. Over the next several days, pay close attention to those situations that are causing you frustration or seem to anger you most often. In a journal, record these frustrations and the situations which brought them about. Once the situation that caused the trigger in you has passed, see if you can specifically identify what caused the trigger. Be careful not to focus on another person's behavior or the situation that is not controllable. Focus instead on yourself to see if you are able to identify something that would allow you to take hold of the emotional reaction you are having.

2. Become purposeful in watching those you coach. See if you can become expert at identifying when their emotions are getting the best of them. Watch for cues in body language and in non-verbal communication. Once you recognize these when they appear, practice calming language and body tone. Sit back, cross your hands and think *calm* in your voice tone. Now get curious. What questions could you ask that would show concern for the coachee so they can reclaim their thinking mind?

3. Make an appointment with your coach and describe what you have learned from the two exercises above. When talking with your coach, focus on the benefits you are experiencing in applying impulse control to your coaching skills. Be sure to include these benefits in your journal.

TEN

Secret #5: Adaptability

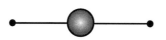

T he best way to describe the Vice President of Engineering, "Sam," is to declare him "A Company Man." Sam was as loyal to the company as anyone ever had been. He always defended the company's position. He viewed doing so as part of a fundamental understanding of his role as one of the firm's leaders, but also because he simply could not think of a time when he genuinely disagreed with a policy or a decision that his company had made.

Sam always looked forward to the coaching interactions with his top people. Marla was definitely one who belonged in that category. It seemed like he and Marla were cut from the same cloth. Marla had developed into a top- performing engineer, one that was very bright and skilled in communicating with contractors on job sites. Sam often thought Marla, since they were so much alike, could have been his daughter. Sam always enjoyed spending time with the top performers on his team, as they seemed to add energy and vitality to his day.

Sam and his protégé had a bit of a drive to reach their first inspection. He looked forward to the longer drives; Sam viewed them as an opportunity to build camaraderie with the people on his team. Shortly after their drive had gotten under way, it was *clear that Marla was disturbed by something. She was noticeably on edge and Sam could feel the tension. Since he and Marla had built such a solid rapport, Sam immediately blurted out, "Marla, you don't seem like yourself." In retrospect, he wished he could take the words back. Alas, the words were out; it was too late.*

"How does someone not seem like herself, Sam?" Marla fired back with a vengeance. "Sam, I am me. I have always been me. I will always be me. It is this company that has changed and not for the better, I might add." The pace of her words quickened and she spoke with energy and passion.

"What is upsetting you, Marla?" Sam pressed.

"I am not sure I can stay with this company," Marla continued. "I have enjoyed my time here, but quite frankly, this is not the only engineering firm in town. I don't think I can work for a company that does not support a balance in work and family life."

Marla's last comment cut Sam deeply. He served on the committee that had developed the firm's policies around work and family balance. Apparently this conversation was going to involve more time than the present drive would allow…

Then the second thought came tumbling out of Sam's mouth, additional words that he wished he had back. "The company policy is what it is." As soon as he heard the words, he wondered why he had spoken them. He really didn't even mean what he said. Sam felt defensive. He knew he should try to clarify with Marla precisely what she had meant by her comments, but he felt attacked. His reaction had been to blurt out a defensive statement.

Sam suddenly recognized that this situation would require him to move in one of two directions. His normal style was not to be terribly inquisitive or curious. Instead, Sam was decisive and action-oriented. He said what he meant and he meant what he said. On one side of his dilemma was a company policy that he himself had helped to create. On the other was his top engineer who obviously had thoughts and feelings about the policy that was causing her to consider leaving the company. Sam hated to admit that he knew that Marla would be leaving his leadership as well.

The fifth secret of an emotionally intelligent coach is adaptability. In researching this book, we spoke with people who had been coached by great coaches. As a result of this research, three forms of adaptability surfaced that dramatically impact the coach's ability to effectively lead.

Adaptability in Style Is Critical in Coaching

We all have natural tendencies in the situations that life presents to us. Some of us shy away from conflict and others seek it out. Some of us much prefer to form our opinions verbally, out loud in the court of public opinion. Others of us require hours of deep reflection, pondering every conceivable option before entering into even the simplest of conversations. If we don't recognize and adapt to these different styles, our expert coaching efforts may make us feel better but likely will do our coachees no good at all.

Much has been written on the subject of personality styles. Should you wish to learn more about these psychological theories, simply search the Internet for any of the assessments below. You will discover a wealth of information that will keep you reading for hours. As a coach, it is important for me to know the personality style of the person I am coaching. Experience has taught me that most of the people with whom I interact are different from me both in personality and in communication style. With even a basic understanding of these styles, I can then be more adaptable whenever the situation calls for it. On the other hand, if I am not aware or conscious of these styles and the differences they may create, I am bound to become stuck in the endless trap of trying to conform others to my own styles. Remember, personality does not change. *We are who we have been created to be.* My role as a coach is to flex and adapt to the styles of those I am coaching, in order to secure the best possible outcomes for them.

Myers-Briggs Personality Assessments

The *Myers-Briggs Personality Assessments* are the result of the work of Isabel Briggs Myers in the 1940's. Her work represented a step forward from the research of Dr. Carl Jung, the founder of analytical psychology.

In her studies, Briggs accounted for four primary ways people differed from one another across a spectrum of two variables. The categorization mechanism that she created allows for 16 different combinations of personality types in which people behave. She labeled these differences across the spectrum as "preferences." These are mental preferences and essentially reflect ways we are comfortable thinking about things.

The first set of these mental preferences are how people "perceive" or absorb information. People who favor clear, tangible data that is useful in the moment are labeled as "sensing." In contrast, people who are more abstract, conceptual thinkers are called "intuitive."

The second set of mental preferences identifies how people form judgments or make decisions. Those who exhibit a natural tendency to make decisions in a logical and analytical manner are classified as "thinking judgers." Their opposites are "feelers," those who show global perspective in trying to establish harmony and the impact that decisions have on others.

The third dimension in the model has to do with "energy orientation." The concept teaches that we can occupy two mental worlds: one that is turned inward toward ourselves and another that is turned outward toward others. People who prefer "introversion" draw energy from the inner world of information and reflection. In contrast, those who prefer "extroversion" are drawn to the outside world. The E-I dimension is often considered to be Jung's gift to general psychology. Unfortunately, this has been widely distorted. This distortion is typically framed as introversion being cast in a negative light while, conversely, characteristics of extroversion are cast in a positive light. This cultural bias frequently leads naturally introverted types to misidentify their primary preference as extroversion.

The fourth preference is a "perceiving orientation" of the outside world. This spectrum contrasts "judging" on one side and "perceiving" on the other. Those with a "judging" style plan and organize. Others who prefer the "perceiving" style possess a more open and adaptable orientation.

As a coach, it is important to know the personality style of the person you are working with and how that may differ from your own style. Bear in mind that, as you assign them tasks, their accomplishment of these will be evidenced in line with these aforementioned personality preferences.

Do not mislead yourself as a coach into thinking that you will be able to change your coachee's personality. That is completely unrealistic. Your goal as a coach is to understand the style of the person with whom you are working and to *adapt* your coaching to reflect your value of his or her personality style. Valuing the coachee's personality preferences will result in far better results for the person being coached while also better aligning your expectations on your coachee's ability to change.

DiSC Assessments

The value of the DiSC is a personality assessment based upon an individual's orientation to task and to expression. This tool is fairly simple to use and, conceptually, is easier to appreciate than the Myers-Briggs Assessment. My reason for suggesting this assessment is that there are only two dimensions to consider along with two spectrums inside those dimensions. This yields four possible outcomes to manage, as opposed to the 16 that are categorized within the Myers-Briggs tool. In my experience as a coach, I have found the DiSC tool to be more useful because it orients me to the preferences around which most of my coaching has been built.

Here are the four DiSC categories:

D=Dominant Type

These are outgoing, task-oriented individuals. These individuals might best be characterized as those who simply GET IT DONE. In being flexible and adapting to this particular style, bear in mind that "D's" need respect and results.

I=Inspirational Type

This category represents individuals who are outgoing and people-oriented individuals. They may best be described as social and fun-loving. In being flexible and adapting to this style, it is important to remember that "I's" need admiration and recognition.

S=Supportive Type

The supportive type of individual is more reserved, yet still people-oriented. This group enjoys relationships and supporting others. In being flexible and adapting with this style, be mindful of the fact that "S's" need camaraderie and gratitude.

C=Cautious Type

Finally, this category reflects those who are reserved and task-oriented. "C's" might best be characterized as those who seek valuable and high-quality information. As you work to be flexible with and adapt to this style, you need to know that this type of individual needs trust and integrity.

Strengthsfinder

The "Strengthsfinder" assessment is a tool created by the late Donald O. Clifton. This tool provides the individual with a glimpse into his or her individual talents. I would suggest that this assessment helps us to understand how people prefer to approach their work.

In the best-selling book, *Now Discover Your Strengths*, Buckingham and Clifton masterfully walk us through the importance of developing people around this talent orientation. This device can greatly assist coaches in understanding how coachees process work along a spectrum of 34 themes or talents. While the task of learning and assimilating the dynamics of 34 talents can be daunting initially, the tool can be extremely valuable in trying to extract better outcomes from coachees.

Clifton and Tom Rath have updated this assessment via a new book, *StrengthsFinder 2.0*. You will find more information online at www.strengthsfinder.com.

Adaptability in Pace Is Vital in Coaching

Each one of us has natural energies we bring to any situation. In coaching, a key priority is to discover our coachees' energy point. In order to do this, we must be prepared to go on a journey with them. The journey is one that focuses on finding the excitement and enthusiasm, not only in what the other person is saying, but also in *how* he or she is articulating his or her concerns. Paying attention to the passion points our coachees bring to our interactions with them is precisely where we will find the most energy for change. At the point where this energy lies is where our success as a coach will be found.

Coaching is also very much about energy. Coaches often enter a situation with their own agenda and a plan for a successful coaching engagement already in mind. They bring preconceived ideas about the behavior they would like to see changed. They already have mapped out the success this will bring to both themselves and their organizations.

Then the coachee shows up and shows absolutely no interest in the topic the coach has prepared. As a coach, what do you do? At this stage of the game, do coaches just abandon their agendas? Should we as coaches always go with the flow of the coachee? This depends, in part, on the coaching relationship.

If you are a professional coach that has been hired by an organization, you may be more tolerant of these diversions, knowing full well you will get to the underlying reason for your coaching engagement. Presumably, you enjoy a perception of time on your side.

If you are in an employee/employer relationship, however, your sense of urgency may be more intense. Perhaps your boss is on your back to quickly change behavior so the organization can move forward.

In either case, paying attention to the pace that your coachee brings to the conversation can reveal a great deal about when and where to employ your agenda. Of course, this is done while keeping in mind that the coachee has needs and brings an agenda into the relationship, as well.

In observing a coachee's energy, coaches watch for three communication basics. First, we measure the speed at which the coachee is speaking individual words. To better understand this, try this little exercise:

Say the word baseball at a normal speed for you as you would use it in a conversation. Now say the word baseball as slowly as you possibly can. The third time, say baseball as quickly as humanly possible!

What did you notice? Presumably, you observed that there are incredible differences in the rates in which we are able to enunciate spoken words and phrases. Begin observing this with the people you coach. Notice the pace with which they use words and how they emphasize individual words. You will become a much better listener if you focus on the pacing differences of individual words.

Secondly, watch for different energies or emphases placed on individual words contained within sentences. Practice this at home in exchanges you have with friends and relatives. You will observe that it is quite common to use different pacing for words as we put conversations together.

Try saying the following sentence by speeding up and slowing down around the word neighbor. Be careful not to confuse a slowed pace with a derogatory tone. We are not listening for tone at this point, just pace.

"Hi neighbor! I haven't seen you in a while. How have you been?"

Tone is the third listening energy. Placing different tonal emphases on words changes the dynamic of the sentence completely. Merely by using a *friendly* emphasis on the word neighbor in the above example can completely change the energy over a *negative* connotation.

Be cognizant of the energy your coachee brings to a conversation. By tuning in to an awareness of words and emphases, you will pick up on subtleties. In that way, you will be able to assist your coachees to maximize the energies they bring to their relationships.

Adaptability in Managing Change Cycles Is Paramount in Coaching

In some coaching situations, it is not unusual for a client to bring a completely different agenda to the table. This may seem to come from out of the blue. Comfort with change and ambiguity is key.

According to the Center for Creative Leadership, one of the main reasons why leaders fail is an inability to adapt to change. Posing questions that are thoughtful and reflective are essential, yet this may require a multiplicity of demand. Circumstances may dictate that you have many things going on around you. For example, your boss may be on your back. A client is trying desperately to reach you. Sales may be down such that the urgency to increase them may be acute. Even if each of these scenarios is occurring simultaneously, how do you adapt to your current environment so you can be *in the moment* with the person you are coaching? There is a certain skill in altering your feelings, thoughts or actions to understand the perspectives of others. We simply can't coach if we are completely entrenched in our own beliefs. We must be able to suspend judgment of the other person's position and, instead, step into his or her position. As coaches, we don't necessarily need to stay there indefinitely, but we must put ourselves in his or her position long enough to understand his or her heart.

Life is not what you think it is going to be, it is what it becomes. Are we able to adapt and change to accommodate the things that come into our lives, or are we resistant? Many changes and the associated stresses that come with them arise from a failure to manage expectations.

Several years ago, I participated in a training seminar during which one of the primary advocates for change came from an analogy attributed to NHL hockey great Wayne Gretsky, arguably the sport's greatest player of all time. The analogy started by highlighting the fact that change occurs in a hockey game literally thousands of times. One second the puck can be directed down the ice by one player and, the next, a member of the opposing team may gain possession and take the puck in the opposite direction. Hockey is a very fast-moving game! Gretsky's take on all this was to advise his teammates not to worry about where the puck is, but rather "skate to where it is going." This is a great mantra for change.

I notice this often when coaching my son's recreational soccer team. These twelve- and thirteen-year-old kids tend to flock together to wherever the ball happens to be on the field. Unless, however, you happen to be the fastest person on the field that day, you will lose the battle for the ball most every time. My fellow coaches and I teach the kids not to worry about where the ball is "in the moment" but rather to think about where it is going so as to get their bodies there as fast as possible.

The Value of Adaptability in Coaching

As a coach, you really must think like this. Your effectiveness in coaching relies upon your presence of mind to know where your client is *in the moment* and then to adapt to where he or she is going to be next. This is the skill of *anticipation.*

Initially, this can be a rather intimidating place for a coach. We coaches can become lulled into that comfortable place where our client conversations *stay* in the moment. For me, personally, the only things that stay absolutely constant in my life are my moral convictions and my guiding principles. Virtually everything else is subject to change. As a coach, it is imperative that I am aware of where the conversation is headed with my clients.

Developing your coaching skills so that you are adaptable in style, pace and managing change cycles will translate into greater success with those you coach. Consider practicing the exercises below to enhance your own adaptability as a coach.

Adaptability Exercises:
1. Search the Internet to find one of the many personality or strength-based assessments. Ask your spouse or significant other to do the same thing. Talk about the similarities and differences you observe in your styles. Become a student of yourself; in so doing as a coach, you will become more comfortable in parting with your fixed positions. You will also be able to better focus your efforts on those being coached.

2. Select a person with whom you have a frequent association. Capture your observations in a journal or notebook as they relate to the pace, tone and emphases of the words and sentences this individual uses. A coach very much needs to be a student of conversation. By paying attention to these nuances, soon you will be able to recognize the energies being brought to different parts of conversation.

3. Develop your ability to anticipate. Dust off your old checkers or chess set. Sit down with a young person. If you don't have a young person handy, borrow one from a friend or relative. Your assignment is to play the game with the child. *(This is a good thing to do, regardless of the skill you are working on in this exercise!)* Your focus on the game isn't winning the game, but is anticipating your moves. Consider not what your next move should be, but what two moves ahead ought to be. Do this after your opponent makes a move, by thinking about what your move should be, then what will their response is likely to be, and finally what would your move be in response to that. At first, this may seem difficult to you. You may even choose to use a pencil and paper at first so as to better see your options. The point is that you are developing your anticipatory skills. As you get better at the checkers or chess games, bridge out to those you coach. Be prepared for the conversation to go *anywhere* your coachees may want to take it. When your coachees feel secure in their needs being met, your agenda will be successful.

Secret #6:
Empathy

A number of years ago, Jon realized that his organization needed to enter the strategic investment market. *After searching for several months and enlisting the services of a headhunter, the executive team was ready to make an offer. Jean's credentials were impeccable: dedicated to family, strong personal values and a proven track record at a Wall Street investment firm. As Jon drafted the offer of employment letter, he had no doubts that Jean was the person to build this book of business for the bank.*

Jean's first year was like any executive honeymoon, full of introductions and networking events. Not until sometime during the second year did Jon realize that something was not quite right. Jean had started to create silos in her organization that were leading to a "we verses they" culture between her group and other parts of the business.

Jon engaged a qualified emotional intelligence coach for Jean through which she received some anonymous feedback via a 360-degree evaluation. Jean listened to the feedback and the coaching, but did not see a need for change. She had been successful on Wall Street, so why should she change? After all, she had been brought in to start a new business unit, not make lifelong friends.

Within six months, it had become obvious to Jon that Jean was not going to respond to coaching. She continued to create dysfunction within the organization. Then came the deciding event on one particular day. While addressing a group of mid-level managers, Jean made a public statement criticizing her boss, the COO, and a judgment call that had been made.

It was clear that Jon was going to have to coach Jean out of the organization. Jon called his own coach on the phone to ask if they could meet. Jon needed to clarify his thoughts on the business reasons for the decision, as well as how to be firm. At the same time, he wanted to be empathetic with Jean.

The sixth secret of an emotionally intelligent coach is empathy. Defined as placing yourself in someone else's position, empathy is critically important to your coaching effectiveness. This definition, however, is severely lacking in emotional commitment to the relationships in which we are to coach. To those of us who are coaching and leading others, empathy is about entering into others' situations. Moreover, this process should entail forgetting ourselves and what we may feel and think at the moment by exclusively focusing upon the situation in which our coachees find themselves. Actively engaging in what it may feel like to be that other person also demonstrates that we genuinely care.

Think of empathy in a coaching relationship as the gift that keeps on giving. If you show empathy to the person you are coaching, he or she will feel listened to and valued. In turn, he or she will value your listening skills. Typically, this motivates him or her to want to give you his or her best efforts in return. If you are accusatory or demanding in your relationship with the person, however, you will get exactly what you are asking for…no more, no less.

In preparing this chapter on empathy, I found myself sitting in a local coffee shop one day while collecting some of my thoughts. Seated at the table next to me was a pharmaceutical sales representative and her manager. The manager was giving her an extremely difficult time because her paperwork had not been completed and submitted on time.

Rather than demonstrating any empathy with the sales person by trying to understand the barriers she faced in completing her reports on time, he told her he did not care what her excuse was. He made it clear that the only thing that mattered was for her to meet his deadlines. The sales rep explained that she found it difficult to comply. She mentioned that she always left her house very early in the morning so as to get to the hospital to see her first customer by 7:00 am. She continued by explaining that she didn't return home until 6:00 pm. After preparing dinner for her new husband, taking care of necessary details around the home, and then exercising, she commonly turned in for the evening around midnight. She repeated this entire scenario virtually every day.

Her manager could not have cared less; he simply was not interested in any part of her story. The sales professional could sense his lack of caring and said, "Just tell me what you want me to do."

To this, her manager replied, "Get your paperwork in on time and respond to emails within 24 hours."

"To do this," she said, "I will need to spend only six hours in the field seeing customers and two hours getting my paperwork in on time."

"Fine," he said. "Just get it done."

Think about this for a moment. This manager, rather than trying to understand where his young salesperson was coming from or what it might be like to be her, didn't even try to empathize. He had his own agenda. Rather than trying to help the young person by being empathetic, he showed virtually no care or concern. Did you catch the fact that, in this case, the manager sacrificed sales for paperwork? By demonstrating empathy, the manager could have coached his rep to complete the paperwork on time while also putting in a full day in the field calling on customers.

In coaching, if we want to be heard and understood, then we need to listen for understanding and meaning.

Imagine this scenario: *A friend of yours was explaining to you a difficulty that she and her husband were having:*

"Our youngest daughter is causing us fits. She is showing a tremendous lack of respect towards both of us..."

Now, you know the parents to be fine, upstanding citizens and of the highest moral and ethical behavior. No one in the community could say a bad thing about either of them. Yet, for some unknown and mysteriously cosmic reason, the daughter of this highly principled couple showed no public or private respect for the parents.

What are your thoughts about the above scenario? Where does your mind take you in thinking about this? Do you find yourself going to the same place as the sales manager in the story above, just thinking about yourself and what you might do? Can you exhibit any empathy, caring or compassion for your friend and the situation in which they find themselves?

Here are some potential responses we hear from people when we pose this question:

- *Sounds like me; I thought I was the only one with a child like this...*
- *This is typical behavior from the last birth order child...*
- *Fine and upstanding parents in the community, but what are they like at home...?*
- *I know these parents; they don't deserve this from their child...*
- *Every once in a while two great parents get a bad kid...*

Can you simply focus only upon what the other person is saying without having any regard for what you are thinking or feeling at the moment? Pay attention to the words and the emotions (or pain, in this case). How can you suspend judgment of your thoughts for the moment so as to better connect with others around you? How good of a listener are you? Beyond words, can you listen for meaning and emotion?

As I have worked on the empathy efficiency in my own coaching practice, I have noticed something quite interesting. Every conversation is really made up of three sub-conversations that I must manage as a coach. I have control over two of these sub-conversations; I have influence over, but no control of, the third. However, it is how I deal with this third sub-conversation that will determine my success as a coach.

The first controlled conversation is the one I am having with you. It represents the dialogue that occurs when two people are trying to communicate with each other. Included in this are the spoken words and nonverbal signals sent between people when they are in conversation with each other.

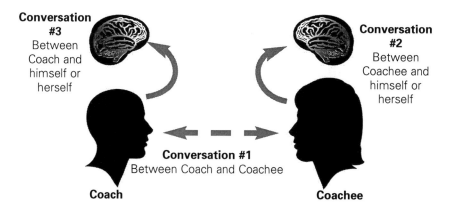

Conversation #3
Between Coach and himself or herself

Conversation #2
Between Coachee and himself or herself

Conversation #1
Between Coach and Coachee

Coach   **Coachee**

The second conversation I control is the one I am having with me. The internal self-talk that goes on as I judge what others are saying while they are saying it is the conversation that inhibits empathy. This conversation focuses the thoughts and feelings on ourselves rather than those we are to be coaching. Hear me when I say that this *second* conversation should not be about us as coaches. Rather, it should be about our coachees or clients. In order to be able to dial into what the coachee is saying, we must find a way to suppress this internal conversation that we so often have with ourselves. If we can suspend our own needs to be right, to be heard, or to be listened to, then we can focus on the other person's needs and desires. This is much easier said than done, especially in the heat of battle. Make no mistake, however; we need to suspend the conversation that we are having with ourselves in order to focus on the one we are having with our coachees. This will allow us to better understand where they are coming from without inserting our own personal biases. Typically, we are then able to see the situation from another's perspective.

Suspending our self-talk also requires us to be aware of the other person's emotions. We must be aware of not just his or her mood, but the underlying emotional needs that are manifesting themselves as moods. This is about appreciating his or her frame of reference. Believe me, we all have our own frames (see *Frames of Mind*, by Gardner) or perspectives on how things evolve. We need to be able to exit our own frames long enough to step into the assumptions of the other person. The rewards for doing so are great. We then will have a better understanding of the perspective the person brings and be able to better appreciate the dynamics at work. If you find yourself unable to appreciate where someone else is in the moment, how can you ever hope to get him or her to where HE OR SHE wants to be?

The third of the three sub-conversations that occur is the one we have influence over but no control. This is the conversation the coachee is having with himself or herself as we are in communication with each other. Clearly, I cannot control what the other person is thinking. As a coach, however, I do have influence over this self-talk that others have with themselves. The more empathetic I am able to be with such a person, the less threatened he or she will feel. By soothing the person's amygdala, I will influence the truth and honesty he or she is able to feel in the coaching relationship. The more I can show him or her I care, the more he or she will trust and value our relationship. As this trust increases, he or she will take great strides in trying to exhibit the behavior change that we all seek.

The Value of Empathy in Coaching

Empathy is about so much more than putting yourself in another person's situation. It's about actually walking in someone else's shoes for a while. Being an empathetic coach means you have to really care about that coachee's situation or problem. This requires an emotional commitment on your part, one that might not always be particularly savory or convenient for you. Yet, without empathy, likely you will never be the coach that you *could be.*

So, if you are not observing the behavior change you desire in your coaching role, work on the exercises below. They will help you get in touch with and improve your own empathy skills.

Empathy Exercises:
1. Tune in to other people and tune yourself out. As you find yourself in conversations with others, suspend your need to listen to yourself. Stop having a conversation with yourself by focusing on the words and the emotional tone that your coachee is articulating. In a journal or notebook, write down any barriers you notice in being able to suspend your judgments of the other person. Where do you think this need to judge others is coming from? As a coach, are you giving yourself a false sense of importance?

2. Find a supporting argument for your coachee. Remember, you are practicing your empathy skills here. As an example, a golfer practices putting; yet, practicing for an hour does not equate to putting every stroke over 18 holes. Sometimes a driver or iron is needed. The point is that we are working on empathy! So find a coachee you trust with a behavior that needs changed. Listen to him or her with the objective of supporting the position he or she takes. You may have a sales person who doesn't want to make cold calls. Fine! Now listen to him or her and ask questions about why he or she feels the way he or she does about cold calling. You are *not* trying to convince him or her that he or she should make cold calls (even though you may know this to be true, remember, this is a practice exercise!). Instead, you are trying to assist him or her in supporting the argument. My experience in using this technique to grow my own skills has been that the person being coached will often see how illogical his or her position is, and then ask for suggestions at the end of the coaching time. It is amazing to me that, when we strike down our positional frames and focus on being empathetic with others, barriers can simply melt away. Performance and the performance of those being coached can *all* improve at the very same time.

Secret #7:
Communication

The seventh and final secret of an emotionally intelligent coach is communication. For coaches, this is all about expression. Communication deals with the way you express your words and can also be used to help your coachees express their thoughts more effectively. Do you have your full thinking mind available to you when you communicate? The thoughts and ideas you communicate coincide with the intellectual side of your brain; yet, what matters most in the conversation is how the message is received. Successful mastery of this efficiency is demonstrating an ability to clearly express both your thoughts and your feelings. It gives you the courage to say what you mean and mean what you say. You are able to produce clarity in your thoughts and to know, with conviction, that what you have said is exactly what you meant.

Within the realm of communication, we must take a non-defensive posture when we listen and when we speak. Yet, how often we violate this critical principle! What would it take for you to listen, without automatically trying to defend your position all the time?

In any such communication, there are several questions to consider: What is the emotional tone of what you are trying to say? Is your instruction adequate? What assumptions are you making that the other person may not be privy to? How do you air your grievances? Are you personal in disagreement? What is your body language saying? Are you clear in your thought expression, or is emotional tone taking over the communication process? How able are you to express your logic so that you can stand your ground?

Let's focus on three important communication strategies you can use in coaching to observe and make necessary changes. The strategies below are consistently observed in great coaches.

Coaching Communication Strategy #1:
Change your "but" to an "and"

One of the most significant communication traps that leaders find themselves in is that of not clearly expressing what they think and how they feel. Most often, this is observed when leaders are coaching. In setting the stage for behavior change, leaders typically give some feedback. If behavior change is desired, there must be something that the coach believes the person could change in order to effect a better outcome. In this situation, the coach views feedback as a gift, yet the coachee interprets the feedback as a weapon. How can this be? How is it that something so useful and that is intended for good, instead, is perceived as a brutal, blunt-force object?

The initial culprits are the feedback models many managers have been taught. Many of these models teach us to start by saying something positive so that the person will be nondefensive and, hopefully, more accepting of the critical feedback we really want to convey. Such a conversation starter might go something like this (Jim is Tanya's boss):

Jim: "Tanya, you did a very good job getting that spreadsheet in on time, *but* the quality of your work could have been improved by using a pivot table."

You may be thinking to yourself that you would never say such a silly thing. As I write this chapter, I have observed this behavior ten times already this week in interactions I've had with professionals. *Would you believe it's only Tuesday?!* The point is that this happens more frequently than you might think. Watch yourself. Be self-aware of this behavior trap. Count how many times you catch yourself using the word "but." Using the word "but" is our way of rationalizing our feedback comments. It's a way of protecting ourselves while not going too far. Problem is, it also makes communication very unclear and causes people to be unsure of what you really mean. Why spoil it with a negative BUT? The "but" denigrates the compliment. Everything you were hoping Tanya would get out of the compliment ends up being completely lost.

The word "but" affects and confuses the clarity of your message. Often, I have observed organizations that utilize this "compliment, *but* criticism model." From our coachee's perspective, the word *but* might better be thought of as *BMQ: Better Move Quick! Because the boss is giving me a positive, what he or she really wants to do is slam me up against the wall!*

Here's what actually happens from Tanya's perspective. She hears Jim talking:

"Tanya, you did a very good job getting that spreadsheet in on time, but…" (*Oh no, here it comes! I'd better get out of the way. That was a compliment and now I know I'm going to get criticized for something I did. Maybe it wasn't me. Maybe it was Sally. What could it have been? How can I position this so it doesn't look so bad on me? I know I will justify or rationalize my behavior. If I give a good enough reason why I did what I did, Jim won't know what to say. Maybe he will just go away.*)

What did Tanya miss? She missed what Jim was saying. She missed her development. What her boss had to say actually might have been something good for her; it may have been a useful comment. The problem, however, is that she did not stay engaged in the conversation because she thought she was going to get hit by the *"but."* Tanya was caught in the third conversation outlined earlier. She was having this conversation with herself and, in so doing, tuned Jim out. She missed any feedback, instruction or advice Jim was trying to convey.

In Tanya's case, everything positive that the manager intended to communicate to her about the on-time completion of the spreadsheet was lost. The supervisor could have conveyed a number of very complimentary comments to Tanya about finishing the project on time. Why did Jim stop with such a short compliment? Why not tell Tanya all of the benefits to her, to him and to the organization for her behavior? The point is that when it's time to compliment a staff member, lavish it upon them and permit them to enjoy it! Pause for a moment to let the words sink in. Let the employee even have the next word. Had Jim done so, he may have heard a response from Tanya like, "Thanks, Jim. That means a lot to me!"

Often, you will discover an unexpected benefit when implementing this technique. When an employee like Tanya, for example, is showered with praise for what she has done correctly, she will often come back to ask if there is anything she could do better. At that point, the door is *wide open* to share the development comment. Even when an employee doesn't ask how to improve upon what he has done, he is in a better position to receive whatever constructive criticism that his manager may wish to share. Why? Because that employee feels appreciated and valued. Sincerity is key in this; you have to mean it. And if you mean it, then say it like you mean it! Allow your people to enjoy those words of praise and success.

As you work on catching yourself saying BUT and changing your own behavior, there is a simple strategy you can use: change your BUT to AND. Here's an example of how this works:

"Tanya, you did a *very good* job completing that spreadsheet on time...*and* do you have any thoughts on the use of pivot tables as a way to improve the quality of the work?"

The word *"and"* does not take away from the power of your compliment. Using AND allows Tanya to be a partner in the solution rather than putting her on the defensive. She actually gets a chance to participate in the development instead of feeling like she is being told what to do.

Coaching Communication Strategy #2:
Nondefensive questioning
Turn the powerful questions you need to ask into discovering how people feel. This is the nondefensive approach to questioning. Utilizing this technique involves asking a question while not thinking about yourself in the communication process. Instead, it requires focusing on what might be the needs of the other person.

In my role as a sales manager for a Midwestern pharmaceutical company some years ago, I observed how well this strategy worked. Sales representatives always wanted to ask good, probing, open-ended questions of the customers. The exceptional sales professionals understood that people (in this case, physicians) buy on emotion and then justify with logic. In the sales process, many of the questions that were asked by the sales professionals actually were articulated in the form of a statement. They were meant to lead the potential customer to a particular place that the sales person wanted the customer to go. Typically, the sales professionals were not thinking at all about the needs of the customers, but rather their own needs. This is not an uncommon situation in the sales process that occurs each and every workday of the year! The reality, however, is that our *needs* are linked to our *emotions*. So in order to truly ascertain what a customer needs, it is essential to find out how they are feeling. Discovering this is the key to the start of a mutually beneficial and long term relationship with customers. Here is an example of how this might look from the perspective of a salesperson, with space for you to consider and write down your own example:

"Statement" Questioning: "Doctor, what is your treatment regimen when treating XYZ disease?"

"Feeling" Questioning Alternative A: "Doctor, what are your fears when you treat a patient with XYZ disease?"
"Feeling" Questioning Alternative B: "Doctor, what concerns do you have when deciding how to treat a patient with XYZ disease?

Your Turn: Take a moment to think of another "Feeling" alternative for the above "statement" question and write it in the space below.

_____

_____

_____

Share your response with us at: *www. IntegratEI.com.* We will post it on our website so that others can share in your wisdom.

Now let's consider this kind of questioning in a coaching relationship. Below you will find a short dialogue. Read through it to see if you can recognize the Statement questioning. When you find it, turn it into a Feeling question. (Examples are provided later in this chapter.) I encourage you to give some thought to and complete this exercise. While it may appear very easy for some of you, many of my clients actually find this a difficult exercise. Practicing this exercise *will* lead to improvement, so let's get started:

Ivan manages a staff of eight marketing professionals. Ginetta is a member of Ivan's team and consistently has been a top performer in the past. Over the past three months, however, Ginetta obviously has been distracted and is not delivering the quality product that has been her track record.

Ivan: "Ginetta, how are you doing today?"
Ginetta: "Ok, I guess. Really busy, so I'd better get to work. I have some scheduling things I must get out by the end of the day."
Ivan: "Yeah, I need to talk to you about that."
Ginetta: "Really? Why? Is there a problem?"
Ivan: "No, not really (he's lying and Ginetta knows it). But

(there's that "but" word) you have always been a top performer in the past, but (here we go again) it seems like your schedules have had more errors than in the past."

What did Ginetta hear? How would you be feeling if you were Ginetta right now? She is probably feeling the same way you are. This is what we call a "double BUT." Instead of being clear on his initial communication, Ivan (who obviously has a problem with Ginetta's scheduling) tells her that there is no problem...then says there is a problem. This looks like the Oreo cookie of conversation: a thin layer of complement between two thick problems!

How would you change what Ivan said in order to effect a better outcome?

_____

_____

_____

Rephrased, perhaps a more positive response could look something like this: *"Yes, Ginetta, there is an issue I want to talk about with you concerning scheduling and before I get to that I was wondering if you have any concerns about the scheduling processes?"*

Such an approach leaves the door open in your line of questioning so that Ginetta doesn't feel attacked. Instead, she feels like she can offer solutions to the issues at hand. You may just be surprised at what you learn.

Coaching Communication Strategy #3: Nondefensive listening

Isn't this easier said than done? We all know how important listening skills are. My guess is that most every book you've read on coaching or communication and every workshop on those topics you have ever attended have covered the topic of listening. Typically, listening is treated like a bank account where you make deposits before you can make a withdrawal: *you need to listen before you can be heard.* While I don't want to discount the important point of this listening frame, I find it quite impractical. The reason is that we can't control the behavior of the other person. We can only control ourselves and our own behaviors. We simply trust that, if we're using good listening skills, the impact on the people with whom we are communicating will be positive.

In some of the seminars I teach, I use a technique called "Listening Stick." Taken from early American history, some Native Americans would employ such a device when they had a disagreement that was leading to the possibility of war with another tribe. In order to subvert war, tribal chiefs would sit between the armies and listen to each other. Whoever holds the "stick" does the talking. Without the stick, one could not say a word and was required to listen carefully, *until the other chief felt heard!* The stick could be passed for clarifying questions but would go back to the speaker until he *felt heard.*

What does it feel like to you to be heard? Have you ever been passionate about an issue, discussed it with a supervisor or subordinate (not to mention a spouse or significant other), and then left the conversation feeling like you really got your point across? The point is that we must leave our interactions and our conversations saying, "I really understand that person's position better."

Interestingly, this happened to me just the other day. My oldest son came home from college and began his summer job hunt. He had a few interviews but had not landed a job after several days of trying. Instead of listening to him and how he was feeling about his lack of success (see the chapter on optimism for more on this), I launched into a discussion on how important it was for him to be working if he was going back to school next semester. After I began to reflect on this, it occurred to me that my response may have been the most unskillful thing I could have done as a father. Of course he knew how important it was to have a job. Of course he wanted to go back to school. Of course he knew he needed money. I just had a need to be heard on this point. Because of this need, I lost my perspective. I really needed to think of my son and how he was feeling at that moment. I needed to let him hold the listening stick and tell me how he was feeling instead of using my *"talking club."*

I first observed this nondefensive listening when I took my first leadership assignment as a sales coach. I remember working with highly skilled sales professionals, talking about some of the finer points on topics like closing a sale. During a sales call, the salesperson generally did a good job of connecting with the customer and then appropriately explained the benefits of the product line. At times, however, they failed to close the sale. This would drive me crazy! I could see the opportunity right in front of them, yet they would not take it.

The question is, what should I have done? As with my son, what I should have done and what I did were often different. I should have taken more of a nondefensive posture in listening. What I found myself doing was trying to convince a sales professional of the merits of closing a sale. When I reflect upon these experiences, it almost makes me laugh. What true, proven sales professional does not understand this? The reality is that skill was not the issue on the part of my sales representatives. Instead, there was emotional behavior that prevented the outcomes that I sought. My job as coach should have been to explore this through nondefensive listening. Instead of trying to make the point of the importance of closing each sale, I should have saved my breath. They already knew this.

What are the barriers to listening that get in the way of effective communication? What are the barriers that prevent us from being nondefensive listeners? Four distractions are described below, distractions that all coaches encounter in coaching situations:

Pride Distraction

Taking a fixed position, often prior to the conversation starting, is characterized as pride distraction. This is easily characterized as someone who already has made up their mind on a topic even prior to the discussion. No matter how logical the opposing argument or how legitimate the excuse, pride says "I am right." I often encounter this at the executive level within organizations. People in positions of power feel threatened by having to admit that they may have something to learn in a public forum. What's more, it's logical to conclude that this pride element affects the trustworthiness of a leader. Author Fabio Sala, in his article "It is Lonely at the Top," identifies one of the most profound gaps that exists between leaders and subordinates. Sala makes the case that leaders fool themselves into thinking they are more trustworthy than their teams perceive them to be.

Nondefensive listening exercise:
On a scale from 1 to 10, rate yourself on your pride distraction:

When I am in a coaching situation I find myself									
1	**2**	**3**	**4**	**5**	**6**	**7**	**8**	**9**	**10**
Always taking and defending a position				Sometimes taking a position				Nondefensive listening	

Consider: Is your pride distraction affecting the trust you are building with your team?

Selective Distraction

The next barrier can be described as taking a fixed position once the conversation has begun. Selective distraction means only hearing what one wants to hear. The message that is intended to be communicated is "filtered" and therefore, unheard. Implementing a device like the "Listening Stick" is designed to reduce selective distraction by helping both parties remain engaged long enough to understand what each is trying to articulate in his or her communication.

On a scale from 1 to 10, rate yourself on your selective distraction:

When I am in a coaching situation I find myself		
1 2 3 4	5 6 7 8	9 10
Always being selective in listening	Sometimes selective in listening	Nondefensive listening

Consider: Is your selective distraction affecting the communication you are having with your team?

Judgmental Distraction

This issue is characterized as when a listener is preoccupied with thinking he or she is right in the midst of a conversation with someone else. The listener has already begun the process of defending his or her own position rather than focusing upon fully listening to the meaning and intention of the other person. This is a very common distraction.

Which skill do you need to develop in order to suspend your need to be right or to be heard so that you can just listen to the other person? How can you stay curious in a conversation about what the other person is saying instead of jumping to thoughts about how what he or she is saying is different from what you think? I am not suggesting that you cannot judge whether or not you agree with the person. This is not about accepting what he or she is saying as total truth. It is about suspending the needs you may have for yourself so that you focus on the other person in a way that will enable you to understand what he or she means. Don't assume you know what he or she means. If you really want to develop this skill, you must engage your thinking mind and be curious about what the other person is communicating to you.

On a scale from 1 to 10, rate yourself on your judgmental distraction:

When I am in a coaching situation I find myself									
1	2	3	4	5	6	7	8	9	10
Always being judgmental in listening				Sometimes judgmental in listening				Nondefensive listening	

Consider: Is your judgmental distraction affecting the decisions you are making with your team? Do you have ALL of the information in order to make the best decisions possible?

Impatience Distraction
This type of distraction involves the tolerance level of the other person's position. Typically, impatience distraction is considered to be greatly impacted by time pressures. In coaching, we must recognize our responsibility to take the necessary time to hear the other person out. Should you find yourself finishing the other person's sentences (whether or not you verbalize this is not the point), you may suffer from this particular distraction.

Here's how this often plays out: You are in a coaching conversation. You do not agree with the other person and you know exactly why. Rather than waiting for him or her to finish his or her thought, you don't even hear what he or she has to say. You have stopped listening to him or her and you are just waiting for him or her to take a breath so that you can share your wisdom.

On a scale from 1 to 10, rate yourself on your impatience distraction.

When I am in a coaching situation I find myself									
1	2	3	4	5	6	7	8	9	10
Always being impatient in listening				Sometimes impatient in listening				Nondefensive listening	

Consider: Is your impatience distraction affecting the totality of your conversation? How are you making the other person feel by always finishing their thoughts?

Now that we have covered these four distractions, we need to measure your accuracy in rating yourself in nondefensive listening. Doing so will necessitate inviting the thoughts of a few other people. Your assignment is to find two people you trust and then ask them if they have examples of when you have exhibited less than your best nondefensive listening skills.

While listening to the feedback being given, it is important to practice your nondefensive listening skills. Suspend your need to be right or be heard or be perfect...and just listen. Ask questions about what they mean in the feedback they are giving. Do NOT stop listening until the other person feels heard and he or she feels like you know what he or she means. After (and not a moment before) you have fully listened to him or her and understood what he or she means, then fill in the chart below. Don't take notes while the other person is talking, because it may cause you not to listen as well as you need to listen. Just ask questions. You should have full understanding of what he or she means, so use this information to summarize in the chart below. Then go back to your self-rated score above. Compare the thoughts you have to the examples he or she has given you. Have you overrated yourself as a nondefensive listener? In your most important relationships, where are some opportunities to become a better nondefensive listener?

	Pride	Selective	Judgmental	Impatience
Example 1				
Example 2				

Communication is a vast subject. Certainly, we could

spend a great deal more time discussing how it impacts coaching and leadership. However, I will leave this subject with one thought. I once read a comment by a university professor who philosophically suggested that nothing that one person ever says or writes can ever be fully and completely understood by anyone else in exactly the same way it was intended.

The Value of Communication in Coaching

Barriers like life experience, language, the passage of time, culture, and many other factors, all combine to change or affect the originally intended meaning. If that professor is even a little correct, we must recognize that communication is already fraught with many challenges and distractions. Adding our own distractions, like those described in this chapter, can often result in disconnects that effectively block meaning and understanding between people. These, in turn, keep us from being the kinds of coaches and leaders that we must be.

As a result, you will find that techniques like nondefensive questioning and nondefensive listening will significantly reduce some of the barriers to communicating with others. Changing your "but" to "and" will make all the difference to an employee who hears very little or nothing of what you say after you use the word "but." Be cognizant of those times when pride or judgmental thoughts serve as distractions to good communications. Implementing these collective strategies will break down barriers and positively impact your ability to effectively coach and lead others.

Communication Exercises:
1. Ask those that you coach to help you identify those times when you use the word "but" in communication. One coachee with whom I work wears a rubber band on their wrist. Each time he uses the word "but," the individual on his team who is on the receiving end of that word gets to snap it. The skill in this is consistently changing your "but" to "and." As you make this transition, you will find yourself saying "…but, I mean. and…" This means you are making progress toward more effective communication!

2. Think about the questions you ask other people throughout the day. Are you asking them from a position of defense? Are you justifying decisions you have made with your questioning? If so, begin to refocus your questioning. Develop a genuine curiosity about others and the positions from which they might be coming.

3. Complete the chart above on nondefensive listening. Work especially hard on obtaining feedback from other people and, as they give it, resist the temptation to explain or justify why you did something. Instead, just say thank you and ask them what you could do to improve.

PART III

Implementing Your Personal Action Plan

So What?
Moving from Intellect
to Action

You will recall that, as stated early on, the goal of this book is for you to unlock in your own life the ability to improve your coaching skills. A key premise of this book for coaches and leaders has been that "emotion drives behavior", hence the link between emotional intelligence and your ability to coach. Emotion also has the ability to influence our thoughts in the moment. The importance of this chapter is to explain the impact of our emotions and, hopefully, to help initiate some behavior change. Being aware of emotions and of the impact they have on thought is not enough. Recognizing our thoughts is also not enough. We must take action. This critical chapter is designed to help move you along this important process. You now possess the secrets of an emotionally intelligent coach, so you must take action. Use these secrets to unlock whatever barriers to coaching and leading you may face.

After reading and pondering these seven secrets, likely you've noticed areas in which you'd consider yourself to be fairly strong. Probably, you've noticed others where you could improve. You have read a few things in this book that, no doubt, you've heard or seen before. Hopefully, you have tripped over one or two new concepts as well. The question becomes, regardless of whether the information is new or old to you: *How can I be better in a leadership moment using my coaching skills?*

The fact is, you are at a crossroads. You've come to a point where inaction meets action. You get to decide which way to go. You can look behind you to see where you've been; certainly, you've done some self-reflection in this book. More than likely, you've been able to relate in some ways to the stories and illustrations in each chapter. You have what you need to perform as a coach. You can only turn to the left or to the right.

Choosing to go to the left would be analogous to the metaphor that you'll always get what you've always gotten because you're going to do what you've always done. As an executive coach, I'm okay if you choose the left. I just want to make certain you have your full, thinking mind when you choose. For those of you who choose the left, you can skip the rest of this chapter and go directly to the last chapter. Choosing a left turn means you are taking an inactive approach to leading. You are leaving this topic of EI and integrating coaching skill to a matter of thought and intellect only.

Should you, instead, choose to turn right, the road ahead is actually before you. However, you are going to encounter some turns and curves along the way. To make your journey as smooth and safe as possible, I've developed an action tool at the end of the chapter to assist you. Here's how to use this tool. You will notice that the each of the secrets of an emotionally intelligent coach are listed down the left hand column of the action tool below. Across the top are the following four columns:

1. What I Want to Work On – Conduct a self-assessment on your abilities with each of the seven secrets. Review the seven efficiencies as well as the exercises in those seven chapters. Rank yourself on a scale of one to seven, with seven defined as "I'm already pretty good at this and to grow would take a tremendous amount of recognition and effort, as well as an expert teacher to take me to a higher level." Assigning a score of one means "I just learned about it or I'm not very good at it, and I probably have a lot of work to do in this area." Now, circle the secret with the lowest ranking, indicating your need to further develop it. Put a box around the secret you happen to be best at, but in which you would also like to improve. Please resist the temptation to select for improvement only those efficiencies that represent your lowest rankings.

For one thing, experience has taught me that you can really only focus on developing one of these at a time. If you simultaneously work on too many of these at the same time, the result likely will be frustration. Often, this leads to a failure to form habits around those things that will make the greatest positive impact for you. Once you have improved your abilities in one secret, others will notice a change in your behavior and give you unsolicited feedback. Then, and only then, should you select the next secret upon which to work.

2. How I Will Know I Have Arrived - Describe the behavior that you would really like to realize in yourself. Start noticing the changes. But don't rest on your laurels. Seek out good reading materials that will push you to continue growing.

3. The Plan - Describe the intentional steps you believe you must go through in order to achieve "How You Will Know." Write your feelings in your journal on how your coaching skills change as you implement this plan.

4. Time Needed for Completion - How long are you expecting this behavior change to take? If you are not absolutely intentional about this process, it won't ever happen. Admit that to yourself. Then, allocate the time you need to achieve this.

At the end of this chapter, we've included a sample action tool to give you an idea of how you could and should implement this to better your own coaching skills, should you elect to do so.

In the next and final chapter, you will learn about the implications of whether or not your plan is successful. You can intellectualize the material in this book, find it interesting or not, and continue your leadership journey. Or, you can develop a plan to improve your coaching skills. The choice is yours.

Sample Action Tool

Seven Secrets	What I Want to Work On	How I Know I've Arrived	The Plan	Time Needed for Completion
Self-Awareness	4			
Authenticity	1	...write my values stmt	...amend values stmt	90-120 days
		...sit with a coach and describe place of conflict in my values		
Impulse Control	5			
Adaptability	6			
Empathy	7	...tuning into others; noticing what I think or feel in the moment	...write observations in journal at the end of each day	...see change in my abil within 2 months ...I'll know I've arrived
Optimism	2			
Communication	3			

Sample Action Tool

Seven Secrets	What I Want to Work On	How I Know I've Arrived	The Plan	Time Needed for Completion
Self-Awareness				
Authenticity				
Impulse Control				
Adaptability				
Empathy				
Optimism				
Communication				

FOURTEEN

Integrating EI Skills into Your Leadership Style

Your leadership style is *not* your personality style, yet people typically become very frustrated when you try to change their personality. They are who they were created to be. Personality assessments like Myers-Briggs and DiSC are commonly used to characterize and differentiate between various personality types.

As was mentioned in the first chapter of this book, I believe that we are fearfully and wonderfully made. We are all made the way God made us and in His image. So who are we to try to change someone's personality? That is a mistake that coaches commonly make. Have you ever had this thought about someone else you were coaching or leading? *Hmmm…you're a passive type of person, but I really need you to become an assertive type of individual in order to better do your job?* What if that's not who that person really is?

First of all, integration of emotional intelligence is not about changing one's personality. It is about using coaching as a leadership tool such that, no matter what the Myers-Briggs assessment reveals one's personality to be and regardless of how the DiSC tool labels someone, leadership skills may be developed and enhanced. While Myers-Briggs is about preferences and how one prefers to act in the world, emotional intelligence (as it relates to coaching) is an understanding of oneself for the purpose of serving others.

Within personality type resides this attribute called competence. Coaching skill is driven in effectiveness by the efficiencies that revolve around emotional intelligence. These efficiencies are personality-related characteristics that *can* be worked on. These efficiencies represent traits that *can* be developed. If you're a very driven person in your coaching, are you able to recognize when you are driving too hard? Are you able to understand when you're not listening? That's the essential application here. That's what I really want to help you to see and understand. We shouldn't want our coachees to be anything other than who they were created to be. We should want them to be the best within whom they've been created to be.

An example of this in a marriage relationship might be characterized like this: I'm pretty much a driven personality, and I also wear my emotions on my shirt sleeve. My wife is a fairly reserved person, so when she says to me, "Scott, you need to listen to me more. I don't want you to solve everything and I don't want you to fix everything. I just want you to listen to me more." That doesn't mean that I'm going to change my personality, or that I'm not going be my fiery self with all of my emotional qualities that I wear on the outside. What it means is that I have to recognize the behavior and possess the self-awareness to say, "Does this behavior serve me right now in the moment? Is this the best choice that I have?" That's the point. The reality is that I'm going to be emotional because that's who I am. Yet, how do I take who I am with the personality that I have and still get the behaviors and the outcomes that are needed? My wife is not asking me to be different, but she is looking for my most skilled response.

To further illustrate this principle: there are times when people who are introverted appropriately ask themselves, "Do I need to be a little bit more passionate around this?

Do I need to adapt? Do I need to be more flexible? Do I need to flex a little bit inside of who I am? Is this behavior serving me?" That's the question. If it is and I'm happy with that, then I have my full thinking mind, and I will get the desired outcome…whatever that behavior is.

While we aren't changing personalities and we are not asking introverted people to magically become extroverts, we must recognize that there are times when emotional intelligence can be changed and improved. In my experience, the best place to begin developing emotional intelligence is in a personal leadership course. Such a course will teach you how to create and use a structured personal learning map in beginning the process, as well as elevate your self-awareness to a new level. The most holistic course with which I am familiar is conducted by the Institute for Health & Human Potential. Information about their resources may be found at their web site: www.ihhp.com. This institute offers the best and most robust training across a vast number of competencies that I've encountered. The program starts with 360° feedback. This instrument necessitates feedback from people you work with, from peers, from subordinates, and from your boss. You will receive feedback from friends, as well as family. The next step is to attend a training course to learn how to use that 360° feedback. Feedback is a gift. People are giving you a gift to help you improve. There should never be retribution for someone giving you a gift, no matter how much the feedback may, in fact, hurt at the time. My experience is that those who offer feedback do so in all honesty and all sincerity in order to help you become a better person. So, this training process is an important first step.

After completing such a course as the one referred to from IHHP, should you really desire to become proficient in your coaching and leadership skills, you will need a coach. If you attend a training course, likely you will return from that experience and share with a friend or colleague some of what you've learned about yourself. You may even make a statement about how you really need to enhance one or two skills in a particular area. That is a very valuable and natural course of action in your coaching development journey. I would suggest, however, that you will very much need someone to observe you weeks and months later. This person may say, "Hey, you're really getting better at that," or he or she might say, "You're still not there yet."

If you don't think that you can obtain that kind of open and honest coaching from a peer or significant other, there are professional coaches that are able to provide this critically important function in your development. If you really want to get better at one or more of the secrets that you have learned in this book, you need to seek the advice of a professional.

Let me paint the picture a bit more clearly: If I'm not feeling well and I have a headache, I may tell my wife I have a headache. She will probably suggest that I take a couple of aspirin or ibuprofen so that I'll feel better. But, if in a couple of days I still have a headache, I need to go to a professional. I need to go to a doctor. I need to seek professional advice on how to take away my pain. This is no different in developing your coaching skills. If you recognize that you really want to work on these skills and you really want to grow, you can take away much from a book like the one you are holding in your hands right now. That's why I wrote this book…to jump start your thinking!

If and when you reach a point, however, where you're saying, "I'm still having trouble with impulse control" or "I'm still having trouble being adaptable in certain situations," you need to start with a training course to delve deeper into skills development and then begin working with a professional. The International Coach Federation is a good resource for finding such a trained professional. The ICF website is located at: www.coachfederation.org.

As you integrate emotional intelligence into your own personal leadership style, there are times when you will need to be direct. There are times where a leader has to take charge and tell people what to do and when to do it. The distinction I want to draw within the context of coaching, however, is this: In your leadership style, are you aware of what steps to take? Are you aware of when is the right time to have a commanding control? When is the time to be decisive? When is the time to coach? When is the time to be submissive? The answers to these questions make a critical difference in becoming the skilled leader that those around you need you to be.

The philosopher Aristotle is credited with suggesting that it's not getting angry that is the difficulty, but rather it's getting angry at the right person for the right reason at the right time. *That* is what is difficult. If you think of the brain as a circuitry, there are typically two outcomes that occur in such a situation: a) stop and redirect your behavior or b) stop and just break the circuit. Grandma told you to take a deep breath, and she was right!

We often use the example of driven leaders who display anger and then blow up. Yet, it is important to recognize that the opposite behavior can create similarly destructive results. When managers and supervisors ignore an employee because they "just can't deal with that today," then the relationship is altered and productivity is compromised. By the same token, this is another area where one needs to be prepared to exhibit their best skilled response.

The rewards that await you if you commit yourself to this personal journey are vast. You will become the kind of leader that others need you to be. You will be more present with people at those times when they most need you.

Let's face it. Leadership is easy when there is no crisis. It is not hard. Anybody can do it, right? I have a client who is an executive at a Fortune 1000 company. He walked in to his sales meeting one day after we had a session together and announced, "Guys, when sales are up and things are good, quite frankly, we could do your job with a spreadsheet. That is not when I need you. I need you when times are tough and when things are down."

When people's heads are between their legs…that's the

leadership moment. That is when coaching becomes critical. That's why your company pays you what it pays you.
Your value to your organization and the people around
you is when the going has gotten a little rough. When sales
are down, the sales staff doesn't need you to read the sales
report and then tell them they're at 89% of quota. Their
spreadsheets have already told them that. An emotionally
intelligent coach and leader, instead, needs to be in the
moment. Such a leader must take stock of his or her own
self-awareness by honestly asking: Am I contributing to my
team's lack of performance? Are the messages I am convey-
ing contributing to the problem?

As a leader, *this* is where you need these seven secrets.
Leaders must know when to be empathetic and how to be
in the moment with their people. If you pay attention to
these seven efficiencies, you will be better in the moment.
You will be especially effective during times of tension and
complexity in your relationships. You will have more of a
presence that brings with it the opportunity to influence
others positively. You will be able to gather all of the mental wisdom that you've been created with when you need it
most. That's what I want you, as a leader, to have: the ability to choose from all of your available options, not just one
that may or may not serve you in the moment.

Since coaching is a leadership tool, let's take a moment to
consider how it might impact *your* leadership. Envision a
group of people sitting in a room. The person at the front
of the room asks everyone present to think of a great leader
and to think of attributes that a great leader possesses.
Now imagine that it is your name that is spoken. One person speaks up and says, "Pete is adaptable." (Imagine that
you are the leader this group is referring to and, for the
sake of this example, your name is Peter!) Sometimes he's
tough and he's hard and sometimes he knows what it's
like. Sometimes he's flexible and he bends and he knows
where the gray is in situations. He's adaptable." Someone
else pipes in, "Peter is authentic. He's real and you get
what you get. Is he perfect? No, he's not perfect. None of

us are, but he is very authentic and he understands what it's like to just be a real human being." Yet another says, "He knows how to set goals. They're achievable. They're obtainable, and we celebrate them when we finish and we celebrate along the way."

Maybe another person in the room suggests that Pete communicates, that he knows when to compliment and when to put a period on it. He's a very nondefensive listener, and he listens with others' best interests in mind. He knows what it's like to be in another's shoes, like having kids that are sick or a tough travel schedule. And yet another says something about Peter valuing his people so much that even when the chips are down, they know that he is glad to have them on his team. Someone else chimes in that Peter knows when to be mad and when to back off. He knows how to help others think positively and to be resilient in the face of adversity. He helps his people stay in the game and not quit, so they give him their best efforts. Peter seems to be aware of the times that he helps others be at their best for the organization. Wouldn't you like to be described like Peter? Is this not the true meaning of how to coach and lead others? Whether we realize it or not, each of us spends a lifetime building some sort of legacy to leave behind. The legacy we leave behind may or may not be one that we would have preferred. You have a priceless opportunity to make a difference in the lives of the people around you. Someday, these same people may attribute to you some of the same qualities that we've characterized in our example with Peter.

Using coaching as a leadership tool and working on these seven efficiencies will be the big win that awaits you. You are going to be more present. You will be more valued. Implementing these strategies will translate into higher sales and less unwanted turnover. You will enjoy deeper and more meaningful relationships. You will be able to go to the well with people and they will tear down walls for you. They will do things they didn't think possible of themselves. Everything rises and falls on leadership.

Effective coaching, using the strategies that you have learned here, is the leadership tool that can and will help you achieve at the highest levels. Be the leader that you were created to be!

References

Amen, Daniel (2006, July, 31). "Long-Term Stress May Shrink The Brain." *Brain In The News,* Retrieved August 7, 2006, from http://www.amenclinics.com

Ancona, Deborah, Malone, Thomas, Orlikowski, Wanda, & Senge, Peter, "In Praise of the Incomplete Leader." *Harvard Business Review,* 92-100.

Bar-On, R. (1997). *Bar-On Emotional Quotient Inventory: User's manual.* Toronto: Multi-Health Systems.

Bar-On, R. (in press). "Emotional and social intelligence: Insights from the Emotional Quotient Inventory." In R. Bar-On & J. Parker (Eds.), *Handbook of emotional intelligence.* San Francisco, CA: Jossey-Bass.

Barsade, S. (1998). *The ripple effect: Emotional contagion in groups* (Working paper). New Haven, CT: Yale University School of Management.

Barsade, S., & Gibson, D. E. (1998). "Group emotion: A view from the top and bottom." In D. G. e. al. (Ed.), *Research on managing groups and teams.* Greenwich, CT: JAI Press.

Bloom, G, Castagna, C, Moir, E, & Warren, B (2005). *Blended Coaching.* Thousand Oaks: Corwin Press.

Boyatzis, R. E. (1994). "Stimulating self-directed learning through the Managerial Assessment and Development Course." *Journal of Management Education,* 18(3), 304-323.

Boyatzis, R. E., Goleman, D., & Rhee, K. S. (in press). "Clustering competence in emotional intelligence: Insights from the Emotional Competence Inventory (ECI)." In R. Bar-on & J. D. Parker (Eds.), *Handbook of emotional intelligence.* San Francisco, CA: Jossey-Bass.

Bray, D. W. (1976). "The Assessment Center Method." In R. L. Craig (Ed.), *Training and Development Handbook.* New York: McGraw-Hill.

Creswell, Jane (2006). *Christ-Centered Coaching.* St. Louis, MO: Lake Hickory Resources.

Davies, M., Stankov, L., & Roberts, R. D. (1998). "Emotional intelligence: In search of an elusive construct." *Journal of Personality and Social Psychology,* 75, 989-1015.

"Delay of Gratification in Children." Walter Mischel; Yuichi Shoda; Monica L. Rodriguez. Science, New Series, Vol. 244, No. 4907. (May 26, 1989), pp. 933-938.

Druskat, V, Sala, F, & Mount, G. *Linking Emotional Intelligence and Performance at Work*. Mahwah: Lawrence Erlbaum Associates.

Feist, G. J., & Barron, F. (1996, June). *Emotional intelligence and academic intelligence in career and life success*. Paper presented at the Annual Convention of the American Psychological Society, San Francisco, CA.

Flaherty, James (2005). *Coaching Evoking Excellence in Others*. Burlington, MA: Elsevier.

Fleishman, E., & Harris, E. F. (1962). "Patterns of leadership behavior related to employee grievances and turnover." *Personnel Psychology*, 15, 43-56.

Fournies, F. (1978). *Coaching For Improved Work Performance*. Liberty Hall Press.

Gardner, H. (1983). *Frames of mind*. New York: Basic Books.

Gardner, Howard (2007). "The Ethical Mind." *Harvard Business Review*. 51-56.

Goleman, D. (1995). *Emotional intelligence*. New York: Bantam.

Goleman, D. (1998). *Working with emotional intelligence*. New York: Bantam.

Gowing, M. (in press). "Measurement of individual emotional competence." In C. Cherniss & D. Goleman (Eds.), *Emotional competence in organizations*.

Hemphill, J. K. (1959). "Job description for executives." *Harvard Business Review*, 37(5), 55-67.

Hughes, M, Patterson, L, & Terrell , J (2005). *Emotional Intelligence in Action*. San Francisco: Pfeifer

Hunter, J. E., & Hunter, R. F. (1984). "Validity and utility of alternative predictors of job performance." *Psychological Bulletin*, 76(1), 72-93.

Lusch, R. F., & Serpkenci, R. R. (1990). "Personal differences, job tension, job outcomes, and store performance: A study of retail managers." *Journal of Marketing*, 54(1), 85-101.

Malouff, J., & Schutte, N. S. (1998, August). *Emotional intelligence scale scores predict counselor performance*. Paper presented at the Annual Convention of the American Psychological Society, Washington, DC.

Mayer, J. D., Caruso, D., & Salovey, P. (1998a). *The multifactor emotional intelligence scale*. Unpublished report available from the authors.

Mayer, J. D., Salovey, P., & Caruso, D. (1998b). "Competing models of emotional intelligence." In R. J. Sternberg (Ed.), *Handbook of human intelligence* (2nd ed.,).

New York: Cambridge University Press.

McClelland, D. C. (1973). "Testing for competence rather than intelligence." *American Psychologist*, 28(1), 1-14.

McFarland, B (2004). *Dropping the Pink Elephant.* New York, NY: MJF Books.

Murray, H. A. (1938). *Explorations in personality.* New York: Oxford University press.

"Never Listen to Armchair Critics, and other Advice." (2006, November 21). *The Globe and Mail*, p. Business.

"Office of Strategic Services Assessment Staff." (1948). *Assessment of men.* New York: Rinehart.

Orioli, E. M., Jones, T., & Trocki, K. H. (1999). *EQ Map technical manual.* San Francisco, CA: Q-Metrics.

Pilling, B. K., & Eroglu, S. (1994). "An empirical examination of the impact of salesperson empathy and professionalism and merchandise salability on retail buyer's evaluations." *Journal of Personal Selling and Sales Management*, 14(1), 55-58.

Ridnour, R (2002). *Mental Vitamins.* BridgExcel.

Rosenthal, R. (1977). "The PONS Test: Measuring sensitivity to nonverbal cues." In P. McReynolds (Ed.), *Advances in psychological assessment.* San Francisco, CA: Jossey-Bass.

Salovey, P., Bedell, B., Detweiler, J. B., & Mayer, J. D. (1999). "Coping intelligently: Emotional intelligence and the coping process." In C. R. Snyder (Ed.), *Coping: The psychology of what works* (pp. 141-164). New York: Oxford University press.

Salovey, P., & Mayer, J. (1990). *Emotional intelligence. Imagination, cognition, and personality,* 9(3), 185-211.

Salovey, P., Mayer, J. D., Goldman, S. L., Turvey, C., & Palfai, T. P. (1995). "Emotional attention, clarity, and repair: Exploring emotional intelligence using the Trait Meta-Mood Scale." In J. W. Pennebaker (Ed.), *Emotion, disclo sure, and health* (pp. 125-154). Washington, DC: American Psychological Association.

Salovey, P., Woolery, A., & Mayer, J. D. (in press). "Emotional intelligence: Conceptualization and measurement." In G. Fletcher & M. S. Clark (Eds.), *The Blackwell handbook of social psychology* (Vol. 2: Interpersonal Processes,). Oxford, England: Blackwell Publishers.

Schulman, P. (1995). "Explanatory style and achievement in school and work." In G. Buchanan & M. E. P.

Seligman, Martin (2002). *Authentic Happiness.* New York, NY: Free Press.

Seligman (Eds.), *Explanatory style.* Hillsdale, NJ: Lawrence Erlbaum.

Schutte, N. S., Malouff, J. M., Hall, L. E., Haggerty, D. J., Cooper, J. T., Golden, C. J., & Dornheim, L. (1998). "Development and validation of a measure of emotional intelligence." *Personality and Individual Differences,* 25, 167-177.

Shoda, Y., Mischel, W., & Peake, P. K. (1990). "Predicting adolescent cognitive and self-regulatory competencies from preschool delay of gratification: Identifying diagnostic conditions." *Developmental Psychology,* 26(6), 978-986.

Snarey, J. R., & Vaillant, G. E. (1985). "How lower- and working-class youth become middle-class adults: The association between ego defense mechanisms and upward social mobility." *Child Development,* 56(4), 899-910.

Stein, S, & Book, H (2006). *The EQ Edge.* Mississauga: John Wiley & Sons.

Sternberg, R. (1996). *Successful intelligence.* New York: Simon & Schuster.

Thorndike, R. L., & Stein, S. (1937). *An evaluation of the attempts to measure social intelligence.* Psychological Bulletin, 34, 275-284.

Thornton, G. C. I., & Byham, W. C. (1982). *Assessment centers and managerial performance.* New York: Academic Press.

"Want to look good? Make the boss look good." (2006, September 20). *The Globe and Mail,* p. C1.

Wechsler, D. (1940). "Nonintellective factors in general intelligence." *Psychological Bulletin,* 37, 444-445.

Wechsler, D. (1958). *The measurement and appraisal of adult intelligence.* (4th ed.). Baltimore, MD: The Williams & Wilkins Company.

Whitworth , L, Kimsey-House, H, & Sandahl, P (1998). *Co-Active Coaching.* Palo Alto: Davies-Black.

(2007, January 2). "A World of bad bosses." *MSN Money,* Retrieved January 2, 2007, from http://articles.moneycentral.msn.com/News/AWorldOfBadBosses.

Journal